Life Looking Death in the Eye

The Iraqi War as Experienced
by a U.S. Army Contractor

Life Looking Death in the Eye

The Iraqi War as Experienced by a U.S. Army Contractor

Mahir Ibrahimov, Ph.D.

GLOBAL SCHOLARLY PUBLICATIONS

Copyright© 2012 by Mahir Ibrahimov. All rights reserved.

Published by
Global Scholarly Publications

Except as permitted under the United States Copyright Act of 1976, no part of this publication may be reproduced or distributed in any form or by any means, or stored in a data base or retrieval system, without the prior written permission of the publisher.

ISBN-13: 978-1-59267-130-4
ISBN-10: 1-59267-130-6

Distributed by
Global Scholarly Publications
220 Madison Avenue
Suite 11G, New York, NY 10016
www.gsp-online.org
books@gsp-online.org
Phone: (212) 679-6410 Fax (212) 679-6424

CONTENTS

Introduction: Why this book is an essential reading for
    all fellow Americans? ix
(i)   A Universal Story of Encountering Death as a Living
       Specter of Life x
(ii)   Specter of Confronting Global Islam xi
(iii) The Potential Catastrophic Agenda of Endless Wars
       with Muslims xi
(iv) The Significance of this Book xii

Prologue: Deadly Day xvi

Chapter 1: Difficult Decision 1

Chapter 2: Preparing for Departure 2

Chapter 3: Deployment 5

Chapter 4: Assignment 8

Chapter 5: The Realities of War 9

Chapter 6: War Before Iraq 11

Chapter 7: The Problem of Insurgency and Terrorism 17

Chapter 8: Western Stimuli, the Rise of Militant Islam and
    its Implications for Iraq and the Region 25

Chapter 9: The Religious and Ethnic Diversity of Iraq 33

Chapter 10: The Security Situation and Mistakes of
    Coalition Forces 37

Chapter 11: Trying to Become a New American 41

Chapter 12: Planning for a Long Stay 43

Chapter 13: Looking for New Opportunities 44

Chapter 14: Dealing with the Worsening Security Situation 45

Chapter 15: Escalation of Hostage Taking 55
Chapter 16: The Constructive Role of Iraq's Top Shite Leader
    Ayatollah Ali As-Sistani 61
Chapter 17: The Uncertainty of Winning the War in Iraq,
    and Its Global Implications 65
Chapter 18: No Clear Strategy 68
Chapter 19: Financial Motives for Working in Iraq 71
Chapter 20: Security Situation Remains a Challenge 73
Chapter 21: Upcoming U.S. Presidential Elections and Their
    Possible Impact on the Situation in Iraq 80
Chapter 22: U.S. Commanders on the Iraqi Insurgency 82
Chapter 23: No Weapons of Mass Destruction........................ 84
Chapter 24: Combining Diplomacy with Military Operations 85
Chapter 25: U.S. Elections and Ongoing Violence in Iraq 87
Chapter 26: Hardships of the War..................................... 91
Chapter 27: Cultural Differences and Other Problems
    Become a Challenge 93
Chapter 28: Important Logistical Hub 98
Chapter 29: Casual Days Amid the Violence......................... 99
Chapter 30: U.S. Elections and the Bin Laden Factor............... 102
Chapter 31: The Assault on Fallujah................................. 105
Chapter 32: Possible Implications of the Fallujah Military
    Operation.. 109
Chapter 33: The Political Process in Washington and the
    Sitaution in Iraq 112
Chapter 34: Vulnerability of Iraqi Security Forces and the
    Political Process in the Country 118
Chapter 35: Major L.: A True Military Professional in My Team . 122

Chapter 36: January Elections 126
Chapter 37: Sergeant S. 127
Chapter 38: Vacation Time 130
Chapter 39: Going Back to Iraq 134
Chapter 40: Back to Work Amid Continuing Violence 136
Chapter 41: Political Process Amid theViolence 143
Chapter 42: Possible Strategic Implications of the Iraq War 147
Chapter 43: Another Mission Behind the Wire 149
Chapter 44: A Dangerous Mission to the Village 154
Chapter 45: Getting Closer to the Eections 157
Chapter 46: Historical Day and Aftermath 160
Chapter 47: Back to Missions and Day to Day Work 164
Chapter 48: Ashura: Concern for Sectarian Violence and the
    Political Process 170
Chapter 49: On Missions Again Outside of the Base 172
Chapter 50: Difficult Political Process and Continuing Viloence 174
Chapter 51: Trying to get Closer to the Iraqis to Win their Trust 178
Chapter 52: Publicity of the War Experience 181
Chapter 53: New efforts to recruit insurgents 185
Chapter 54: Moving Military Convoys for Logistical Support
    of the Army's Operations 189
Chapter 55: One Year Since I Left Home 192
Chapter 56: The Political Process Moves Forward 196
Chapter 57: Dangerous Mission 199
Chapter 58: Violence Escalates and the First Elected
    Government is Formed 203
Chapter 59: Preparing To Go Home 209

Introduction
Why this book is an essential reading for all fellow Americans?

This remarkable book will transform your heart as it describes the day-by-day world of young soldiers and Iraqi nationals fighting in the Iraq War. Imagine that you are a soldier: having left your family and home, you find a unifying identity in the support system of your army buddies. You are them and they are you. Then suddenly, one of them is shot right next to you; you know that it could have been you. You reach out to hold the dead body in your arms. You feel utterly helpless. Your last resort is take the little hope that you have and try to reach above to the heavens—assuming that there is some kind of supreme power that is listening—and beg for your fellow soldier's life. You want justice and mercy. Then you suddenly listen to the most deafening silence—no response. A gruesome fear overcomes you as you think about who may be next. Suddenly, the question of the meaning of life hits your soul, with the fearsome option that there may be no meaning. John Paul Sartre, the genius of existentialist literature and philosophy, observes, "Life is absurd, and the fact that it is absurd is also absurd." But when one embraces the body of a fallen soldier, one feels divine-like grace and the type of suffering only depicted in art, music, and deep religious poetry. Indeed, death is the most essential specter of all living beings, and it is especially felt at the death of others. In a sense, we do die more than one time.

The story is universal, but it takes place in the world of Iraq, which consists of a rainbow of different societal and tribal complexities. Consequently, the author of this book must be a master of many worlds. To that end, this story is not narrated by a chaplain or a poet. Our author is more than a psychological observer of our Divine comedy; he is a unique master of both Islamic and Western cultures. He feels the existential passions and world views of the Iraqis in-depth, but he also understands Western professionalism, being a linguist-contractor and a scholarly master of languages and culture. He is many things: a PhD, ex-Soviet military personnel, husband, and father. He has tasted the sweetness and the bitterness of life. His story is essential reading for every American.

A Universal Story of Encountering Death as a Living Specter of Life

This book delves into a universal idea that applies to all humanity: the semi-conscious fear that death is the most living reality of life. We especially feel the reality of death in our encounters with the death of others. The more friends die—sometimes in our arms—the more we reach out to the silent sky and heavens for explanations. As living human beings, our immediate feelings of well-being, strength, and peace in our souls depends on our interpersonal ties to others. In war, we hope for security and support, and we reach out to our comrades for connection. Even when we feel this joy of togetherness—when we realize that we are not alone in war—there is still the subconscious specter of death that proves to be the most alive potential reality to cut across our desperate existences. When it hits our bodies, we are troubled in two ways. The first thought: How close am I to death? The second thought: the part of me that was my body has died forever, and I am no longer what I was. The combination of me and my support system has died; I am left alive to drink the sorrow. This feeling of shock and despair is experienced by any whose mother has died. We know that no one talks to us the way our mother does. She was so close to us that we never imagined a world without her, and after her death we never feel the same. This book takes the reader into the very complex being under the specter of death: dying each time a body dies, being shaken in the very core of our existence by the remembrance of sweet lives lost forever, and finally, there comes the courageous and desperate effort of hanging on to life and the desire to go on.

Specter of Confronting Global Islam

Iraq made a majority of Americans aware of the specter of encountering the demographical political dynamic of what may be called "Global Islam." This reality is the second vital aspect of this book's content.

At the projected rate of 1.5% for the period from 2010 to 2030, the Muslim population will make 26.4% of the world's total projected population of 8.3 billion in 2030. The world's Muslim population is expected to increase by about 35% in the next 20 years, rising from 1.6 billion in 2010 to 2.2 billion by 2030. This growth is expected to take place not only in countries with a predominately Muslim population, but also in America, Europe, and Asia. (The Future of the Global Muslim Population Projections for 2010-2030, The Pew Research Center, Jan 27, 2011). *A remarkable feature is that Muslims occupy some of the most strategically important lands, such as the Suez Canal, Mesopotamia, Afghanistan, and Central Asia. In addition, much of world's petroleum, minerals, and raw materials are available in countries that are predominately Muslim. In light of this data, it is essential for the United States' survival to eventually make Muslims our partners in trade. In addition, The People's Republic of China's economy is growing rapidly, often dominating markets that were open to Western exports. In this light, the United States cannot compete with PRC and have a hostile relationship with Muslims. Also, while PRC is focusing on selling more to markets that were previously devoted to Western products, much of the USA's resources are being spent on war.*

The Potential Catastrophic Agenda of Endless Wars with Muslims

Armed conflict with Muslims has been and will continue to have many different types of costs. Let us focus first on the case of Iraq-Afghanistan conflicts. For the young men and women of America, there have been nearly 6,000 deaths, around 43,822 US troops and nearly 70,000 allied troops have been wounded. Estimate for Iraqi and Afghan civilian deaths is up to 137,000. (US and Coalition Casualties in Iraq/Afghanistan, Catherine Lutz, Watson Institute for International Studies, Brown University, June 6, 2011.)

In addition to casualties, there has been psychological damage to the veterans and families of the American military. No price can be placed on these wounds. The economic cost of war has been clearly estimated. Conservative estimate costs of war in the period of

2001-2011 is $2.27 trillion, a large portion of the present 4.39 trillion dollars of the USA's national debt (Economic and Budgetary Costs of the Wars in Afghanistan, Iraq and Pakistan to the United States: A Summary, C. Crawford and Catherine Lutz, Watson Institute for International Studies, Brown University, June13, 2011.) It will take much effort to move a giant, such as the USA's economy, from a war-based industry to a peace industry that can successfully compete in the global market. Another major dimension of war with Muslims is the decrease in Americans' popularity with the Muslim world and the opportunity for America's enemies to use the armed conflict to rally the Muslim masses against America. In the long run, Muslims' reception of America will be very essential for our future trades with Muslims who reside in PRC, which will be the most important economic force in the world. Under no condition in the future will the United States be able to compete with PRC and simultaneously fight more than one billion Muslims. Samuel Huntington is dead, and because of the miscalculation of his clash theories, he also needs to be buried with the realities of both the present and immediate future.

The Significance of this Book

We Americans need an in-depth understanding of the socio-psychology of military encounters with Muslims that depicts the core behavior of Muslim social ethos within the context of confrontation with Americans. Readers need to be able to place themselves in the center of the conflict with a true expert on the Muslim culture. This is an expert who, as a native, feels the heart of the Muslim culture and its people, but is also well aware of Western social scientific methodology and seasoned in different types of military service. Therefore, this book is a perfect solution, as its author has a mastery of Muslim community, sociology, languages, and lifestyle.

Through the chronology and analysis of events, the author successfully gives the reader an in-depth understanding of the culture, politics, and economy of Iraq, a nation that is rich with Muslim history and culture; in fact, Iraq is recognized as the heart of the Muslim civilization. Fellow Americans need to understand Muslims and there is no better way than the virtual presence that the author provides through his detailed description of his time in Iraq.

The real value of this book is the fact that it is written by an insider who went with the U.S. military through all the hardships and realities of the war, especially at its most difficult and unpredictable stage, when the insurgency started to take shape and develop as a well-organized and financed movement. Secondly, the fact that the author is fluent in Arabic and Turkish—the main languages of the region—and is a qualified expert in Middle Eastern affairs gave him an opportunity to base his observations and analysis on his own firsthand experiences.

The book is unique because the author experienced military service in both the former Soviet Army and as a military expert-contractor with the U.S. Army in the war zone. He received a Doctorate degree in his studies related to the U.S. policy in the Middle East.

Dr. Ibrahimov is originally from Azerbaijan. That country is traditionally Muslim, with a majority of the population being represented by the Shiite branch of Islam, but at the same time with a great degree of ethnic and religious diversity—just like in Iraq. But more than seventy years of the former Soviet domination has made the "Islamic factor" a much less significant player in the political, social, and economic life of the country. Also, Azerbaijan is currently one of the most secular and pro-Western countries in the region.

The country's secularization, and particularly its pro-Western orientation, became possible after Azerbaijan—for the second time in its history—gained independence from Russia in the beginning of the 1990s as a part of the former Soviet Union. In 1994, Azerbaijan and a consortium of Western oil companies (including American ones) signed the so-called "Contract of the Century," which laid out the basis for a democratic and independent society with a clear pro-Western orientation.

The Independent Republic of Azerbaijan is viewed by many Azerbaijanis as a logical continuation of the traditions and values of the first Democratic Republic of Azerbaijan, which existed from 1918-1920 and was founded by Mammad Amin Rasulzadeh and his followers. Later, as a result of the military intervention of Bolshevik Russia's 11th Red Army, Azerbaijan was forcefully incorporated into the former Soviet Union as one of its Republics. This lasted until the breakup of the USSR in the early 1990s.

The author of the book was one of the first Azerbaijani high-ranking diplomats to arrive at the newly opened Embassy of Independent Azerbaijan in Washington D.C. After completion of his diplomatic mission in the U.S., he returned to his native Azerbaijan and was offered the position of Vice President of the newly established American University in Baku (Azerbaijan), and was later the President of the Educational Center in Washington D.C. Following this, the author worked for a number of years as a consultant to several multinational American companies. He was also a visiting professor of Modern Standard Arabic at the American University in Washington D.C. While working at the American University, the author also taught foreign languages at different learning centers. Also, before and after his deployment in Iraq, he taught Azerbaijani and Russian to the employees of the State Department and other government agencies at the State Department's Foreign Service Institute.

Later he became the first Army Senior Culture and Foreign Language Advisor to the Senior military leadership. He is responsible for culture and foreign Language strategy implementation across the U.S. Army.

Consequently, the uniqueness of the author's background is a combination of his work experience in the former Soviet Union, independent Azerbaijan and the United States. He was also educated in both Moscow and Washington D.C. He served in both the former Soviet Army as a soldier and as a military linguist-contractor for the U.S. Army in Iraq and was part of truly historical events in that country.

Prologue
Deadly Day

I came back to the unit earlier than usual on that day. The security situation was up and down all the time. We had mortar and rocket attacks several times a day. Tragedy was happening randomly and, unfortunately, we were getting used to it. But the tragedy of June 16, 2004 shocked all of us. We knew that we would remember it for the rest of our lives.

I had just come back from work when I realized that I needed to buy some toothpaste. I was about to leave my place to go to the store when I suddenly felt very tired and decided to lay down for awhile. When I woke up one and a half hours later, I finally left to go to the store. As I approached the building, I noticed a crowd of people gathered around. It was the looks of shock and fright on their faces that made me realize what had happened.

A war is made up of thousands of stories of loss and pain. For instance, I know that after the first round of a rocket attack hit the base on June 16, 2004, a group of soldiers and contractors left the safety of the military store before the typical "all clear" siren sounded. Four soldiers were killed and about 25 were wounded when a second rocket fell.

Sergeant M. was one of the four soldiers killed during that attack. He had just left the internet café, where he had been looking for tickets and hotel space for him and his family. His extended 15-month assignment in Iraq was coming to an end. In fact, M. was supposed to arrive home the following day and be reunited with his family. June 16, 2004 was supposed to be the last day that Sergeant M. spent away from his family. Instead, it was his final day.

A female soldier from his unit was at the nearby calling center when she heard the blast. She rushed to the scene and saw Sergeant M. lying on the ground with a piece of shrapnel lodged in his throat. As he lay there dying, the female soldier pretended to be a medical nurse from the hospital and held M.'s hand, comforting him in his last minutes.

In war, it is possible for there to be stories of miracles mixed in with the stories of loss and pain. As tragic as this incident was, it was a miraculous moment for me. If I had not fallen asleep after work I would have been buying toothpaste at the exact spot where that rocket fell. I could have been one of the wounded or dead. Suddenly feeling tired and falling asleep probably saved my life. I owe more to fate than I can ever repay. When this kind of incident happens you start rethinking your entire life. How and why did I end up in Iraq in the first place? Would another twist of fate lead me to the type of tragedy that I had just barely missed? Or did I think that this kind of incident would never happen to me? The nasty and brutal realities of the war became a part of my year-long Iraqi experience. It was an experience that would change my life forever.

Chapter 1
Difficult Decision

After teaching foreign languages such as Arabic, Russian, Azerbaijani and Turkish for the preceding several years, I received an offer to work as a U.S. Army Contractor in Iraq. Of course, taking this job would drastically change my lifestyle and force me to be away from my family for a long period of time. I knew I did not want to miss out on my thirteen-year-old daughter's most important years. I also knew that she and my wife would worry about me each day that I was gone. After considering the pros and cons, I decided that this opportunity could be one of the most important missions of my life. It would allow me to be a part of something important, something that would enrich me morally and make my life more meaningful. At the same time, after spending many years researching and teaching issues related to the Middle East, I was looking forward to getting to know the culture of the Iraqi people through my own practical experience.

I knew I had to tell my family what I was considering. To them, the idea seemed so far-fetched that they thought I was joking. I explained my reasons and we all eventually agreed that a one-year contract with the U.S. Army would be reasonable. I accepted the job and began the necessary preparations.

After going through many background checks, medical examinations and language tests, I met all the requirements for the position of a U.S. Army Linguist/Contractor. On March 20, 2004, I was one in a group of new employees sent to Fort Benning, Georgia.

Chapter 2

Preparing for Departure

At Fort Benning, we stayed in the military barracks at the CRC (Army Conus Replacement Center) while undergoing further medical examinations and taking immunization shots needed for the Iraqi situation. At the same time, we were undergoing the necessary preparations for our service in the combat area. The survival techniques that I learned during this training stayed with me throughout my service in Iraq. They were especially useful when we traveled to the Iraqi villages on missions. The classes included training on how to protect ourselves from chemical or biological attacks, as well as from the different insects and illnesses of the area. We were taught to drink only secure water provided by the U.S. military in bottles, to shake our clothes and boots in the morning before putting them on to protect against the snakes and other insects, and to take our malaria pills accurately and on time. The classes also included instructions on how to deal with the security situation, especially during the insurgency warfare. For example, we were told to be careful among the crowds of local Iraqi people, to watch their hands and moves and not allow them to stand behind us. And of course, one of the main training maxims was not to go out without U.S. military protection. Later, one of our American linguists of Sudanese origin did not follow that advice. He occasionally went to the mosque and even openly demonstrated his intent to be helpful, giving out money to the poor Iraqis standing nearby. One day when he was leaving the mosque, insurgents brutally cut off his head at the entrance to the holy place. It was a horrible death, and one which we knew could happen to any of us if we did not follow the advice that was given to us.

Fort Benning is one of the Army's central rotation points of departure or return for service members and contractors. Staying there was an interesting experience in itself. Some of the soldiers were returning from Iraq, Afghanistan, Guantanamo Bay, and other places, after being away from their families for a year or more. And others had already been in their second or even third tour overseas. Our experiences were so disparate that I found it very interesting to talk with them about their experiences. They had a sense that they were a part of an important mission.

Once, I met a young soldier who was busy cleaning his weapon. He was smiling and making jokes, expecting to be deployed to Iraq in a few days. Out of curiosity, I asked him if he was afraid of going to a war zone. He quietly replied, "No, I am not afraid because it is better to die from a bullet than from cancer or heart disease." He continued to clean his weapon as he said this.

While waiting for deployment, I shared my room with a young soldier named Chad. Chad was about eighteen years-old, but looked even younger than his age. He had already been oversees with a few assignments and he was now heading to Afghanistan. He had more life experience at eighteen than many have in a lifetime.

I was impressed by Chad's ability to see a problem and easily fix it. For example, I once left a key inside of the locker and accidentally locked it. Several soldiers, including a well-trained Ranger, tried to open or break it, but the metal locker was so solid and firm that no one could get it to open. A little later, Chad came in and asked what had happened. We explained the problem to him and continued brainstorming. But, before we were even able to come up with another means of opening the locker, Chad had taken something from his pocket and popped the locker open. In a minute's time, a teenager was able to do what several seasoned soldiers could not. The Ranger next to me said jokingly, "Be careful with him, he can open any door."

Linguists who were hired to work in Iraq for the U.S. Army had mixed feelings about going to the combat area. Some of them hesitated about going; they gave up and went back home before getting to

Iraq. Those who were more experienced and had already been in a war situation, such as the eight-year Iran-Iraq war, behaved calmly and they planned to stay with the mission for at least one year. However, simply put: We feared for our lives. The majority of us had families back home and we knew that we were going to a real war zone. There were also rumors circulating among the linguists concerning the casualties in Iraq. By that time, the war had already entered the period of insurgency warfare, which made things more complicated and unpredictable in the country. That is why, being realistic, I knew that there was a possibility that I would not see my family again. My wife and daughter were taking my departure so hard that it was hurting my morale. Once, my daughter told me over the phone that my wife frequently cried with worry over my absence. I wasn't surprised to hear how emotional she was. Before I had left, I took care of the insurance matters through my employer. When I tried to explain to my wife what had to be done in the case of my death or disability, she simply burst into tears, tears which I realized she had barely been suppressing for several days. I did not talk about it anymore.

It was the day after my failed talk with my wife that my family saw me off. I was looking at them through the window as they stood watching the departing bus and hugging each other. At that moment, I realized that while I was overseas I would carry not only a fear for my own life, but also a concern for my family back home.

Chapter 3

Deployment

Finally, after one month and five days at Fort Benning, we were flown to Rhein Main, an air base in Frankfurt, Germany. After 11 days in Frankfurt, we were taken by military plane to the U.S. "Anaconda" air base in Iraq. Of the four American linguists on the flight, I was the only one who was not of Kurdish descent from Northern Iraq. As we approached the country, my colleagues got excited. Saddam Hussein's oppressive regime had caused many Kurdish Iraqis to emigrate, leaving behind their homeland and many family members. A Kurdish-American female linguist sitting next to me on the plane said that after being in exile for so many years, she was looking forward to finally seeing Iraq and her relatives very soon.

When we were about to land, the pilot came out and said that we had to wait because of a sand storm at the airport area. My seatmate appeared to tense-up at the pilot's words. She turned to me, and when she spoke her voice sounded shaky.

"A sand storm? I bet there is something else going on that they are not telling us. Something worse than a sand storm."

I spend the next few minutes trying to calm her down. After I had finally managed to assuage her fears, the pilot came out again to remind us about how to use the emergency parachutes. My colleague seemed to forget all of my reassurances; she took a copy of the Koran from her backpack and began to pray. I could hear her as she spoke the holy words in a hushed and desperate voice. While she prayed, she squeezed my right hand with such force that I could feel my fingers tingling from the base of my palm to the tips of my fingernails. Despite her fears—which, I must admit, were creeping into the cracks of my resolve—the flight ends without incident.

We arrive in Iraq on April 21, 2004 and are taken by military helicopters to the country's capital, Baghdad, for further registration. There is no way to confuse this flight with a commercial plane ride. Here, two soldiers flank each side of the helicopter, their weapons on the ready to open fire. There are not friendly skies. Also, because an attack is possible at any moment, the helicopter flies at various altitudes; sometimes we get so close to the ground that I think I could open the door, take a step, and feel the hot dirt ground my feet.

We spend the next few days lodged at the Baghdad Zoo, or at least what remains of it. It was once a majestic place. Located along the beautiful Tigris River, the zoo once housed hundreds of animals: Bengal Tigers, brown bears, lions, exotic birds. We are told that all the zoo animals were either killed or captured by U.S. soldiers after the 2003 invasion. Now, U.S. military forces are occupying this area, which includes the former palaces of Saddam Hussein and his family. Although the zoo is just a remnant of what it once was, the empty green cages that stare at us at every turn are reminders that there was once so much life on these grounds.

After our processing is complete, another linguist and I are asked to don civilian clothing and cover our military duffel bags with black plastic. Then, we are driven in a civilian car to the "Anaconda" air base in central Iraq. In order to get to the base, we must travel down one of the most dangerous roads in Baghdad. We learn, very quickly, that sometimes the safest way to work for the military is to appear as though you do not.

Although the hour-long trip to our assigned area is without incident, we do notice the tell-tale black spots from exploded IEDs (Improvised Explosive Devices) along the road. The black spots, like the pilot's message and the civilian clothing, are reminders that every moment I spend in Iraq could be my last.

At first, we are housed in tents. They are very cold at night and very hot during the day, and our air conditioners frequently break down. They also provide very little protection from the danger of the war zone. One of our soldiers was killed when a mortar round landed on him while he was sleeping; he was killed instantly. In a separate attack, an airman was also hit in his sleep and lost both arms and a leg as a result.

Because of the frequent mortar and rocket attacks, it becomes unsafe to stay in the tents, and we are moved to hardened buildings left over from Saddam Hussein's time. They were part of a former Iraqi army base and are now being used by the U.S. military. Each time I think of this situation, I am always struck by the deep irony of it all.

Chapter 4

Assignment

I am assigned to the Civil Affairs Unit. Our mission is to help Iraqi villages with various projects, such as water purification, construction of schools and medical facilities, medical assistance, etc. It is a hardworking team led by Colonel Z., who quickly becomes a good friend of mine. Colonel Z's ability to remain clearheaded and decisive without losing his affableness earns him my deep respect; he swiftly dealt with life and death issues without losing a human touch. I believe that the respect that Colonel Z. garnered from both the American servicemen and the Iraqi civilians directly led to our safety. In fact, during my time under Colonel Z's direction, we are never attacked by insurgents.

One of the most profound experiences was meeting ordinary Iraqis. Building bridges between the cultures and developing a mutual understanding and even appreciation is one of the most important strategies of the U.S. government; it was and still is an important personal goal of mine, as well. I always tried my best to take advantage of those opportunities that would allow me to travel to the friendly villages and get to know the people. Whether it was a dangerous area or not, precautions always had to be taken—soldiers stationed in each room of the building, and on every street corner and roof within eyeshot. Despite the fear of violence and the extra work that it required, I still believe that these trips served as small steps in the right direction in regards to American-Iraqi relations.

Chapter 5

The Realities of War

While helping the Civil Affairs Unit, I am also assigned to work with the unit that is responsible for setting up military convoys. Basically, we must accompany civilian cargo trucks that are working for the U.S. military. Our presence is vital as attacks on such convoys are happening on a daily basis. During this time, we are working closely with Captain Christopher Sinclare, another pleasant personality who soon joins the circle of friends that I am making during my service overseas. I like his quiet style, his smile, and the thoughtful way that he deals with people in amidst these rough conditions.

My time with this unit coincides with a particularly deadly period of the war. On May 25, 2004, a 31 year-old Turkish truck driver is killed by a roadside bomb. He had just left the base, heading with a convoy to the north, when the bomb exploded. I am asked to look through his personal documents; they are covered in fresh blood. I make the mistake of touching the bloody papers without wearing gloves. The large red droplets seep across my hands and settle into the lines of my palms. It is a strange feeling, knowing that the blood of a dead stranger is on your skin. As I look though the man's belongings, two thoughts crossed my mind. First, one day, another man could be going through my things, with my insides becoming bloody smudges that will be wiped away. Second, thank God that it is not me. At least not today.

The stories of explosions, attacks, and disappearances pile up. Later that month, four Filipino contractors are killed by a mortar attack. A representative from the Philippine Embassy visits the base, expressing concern about the safety of its citizens. Reportedly, many Filipino contractors quit after that incident. The following month,

June of 2004, ends on both low and high notes. On June 27, 2004, two civilian truck drivers are kidnapped. Their fate remains unclear. The following day, political power in Iraq is handed over to the transitional government. Although many view this historical event with skepticism—rightfully so, given the insurgency that intensifies in its wake—it is certainly an important beginning to the long and difficult political process that will hopefully lead to the unity of the country and the flowering of democracy.

Chapter 6

War Before Iraq

My first experience with the army was back in 1974, but it was the army of the former Soviet empire, still in its reign at the time. As a citizen of the former Azerbaijani Republic of the USSR, I was required to serve on active duty in the army for two years. At 18- years-old, I was sent to the Russian city of Volzskiy, located at Akhtuba, the Volga River's smaller arm. Akhtuba is famous as the site of an important World War II tank battle. My father was an artilleryman in that battle which is known as a "Stalingrad battle". The Soviet's win was considered a turning point in the war.

After we completed an intense six-month training program, we were given military specialties. Following my graduation, I was sent to a military base in Kaliningrad, at the extreme Western point of the Soviet Union.

My time in the Soviet Army toughened me physically and mentally. Life as a solider in the Soviet Army was a brutal experience. It was difficult to adjust to living in one of Russia's coldest areas. It was also difficult to adjust to the treatment that Soviet soldiers received. It was common practice for subordinates to be bullied and beaten by commanding officers. I woke up with a very high fever on my third day of training. On that morning, we were supposed to run with full ammunition down a high hill and then climb back up. I tried to get up, but could not; I was too weak. The next moment, I felt a bitter pain across my back and right shoulder. It was Sergeant Prihodko, hitting with his belt and shouting, "Get up! Get up!" Forgetting for a moment that retaliation was not an option for "grunts" like me, I jumped on him. I was overwhelmed by the anger that I felt for this man. How dare he treat me this way, as though I were an animal to be broken? Several other commanders rushed to his aid and pulled me off of him. My punishment for insubordination was a brutal beating by the group of commanders.

Later, in Kaliningrad, we had to spend many hours on the cold waters of the Baltic Sea, providing deployment for the troops on specially designed military pontoon bridges. It was routine for several soldiers to be killed or wounded during these activities.

I completed my service in 1976 and returned to Azerbaijan. The hardships of the army changed me as a person. Before I left, I had attended a medical college. But, after two years of post-army work as a dental technician, I realized that dentistry did not interest me any more. The army had sparked my curiosity. I knew in my heart that I needed to pursue a career that would allow me to learn about other cultures. I started to learn foreign languages and write articles, trying to develop my journalistic skills.

In 1986, I graduated from People's Friendship University in Moscow summa cum laude with a Master's Degree in International Journalism. I also became a Qualified Linguist in English and Arabic. That same year, I accepted a job as an expert in the Executive Committee of the Red Cross of the USSR. I was responsible for coordination and implementation of humanitarian programs within the former Soviet Union. Later, I became a Chief Expert in the League of Scientific and Industrial Associations of the USSR, where I aided in the continued development of economic and trade relations between the Soviet Union and the U.S. and between Canada and Japan. I managed to continue my education at the same time. In 1991, I graduated from the Academy of Social Sciences in Moscow, with a degree in International Relations, which was later equated to an American Ph.D.

Gorbachev's liberalization policy was leading to major changes in the USSR. After a failed coup d'état attempt by a group of Soviet officials, the push for democracy seemed to accelerate.

It became clear to me that one of the most powerful empires in history was coming to an end. Thousands of people took to the streets, demanding democracy and rallying against the Soviet officials who were desperate to save the empire. I was a witness to it all.

In Central Moscow, the Ploshchad Nogina (Nogin Square)—the area where the buildings of the Central Committee of the Communist Party are located—was surrounded by troops on a daily basis. But, this did not intimidate the people. Those who had been kept down for so long refused to be silent. I watched as Lubyanka Square became flooded with people. Groups tried to crash the doors of the KGB building. Stones and bottles were thrown at the windows. "Fascists" was written in black letters across the main door, large enough to be seen from miles away.

I noticed a man who had climbed on top of a statue of Felix Dzerzhinsky, one of the founders of the KGB. He tried in vain to topple the statue, tying it in ropes and pulling at it with all his force. Anyone could see that the statue was too solid to be moved with just ropes and one man's strength. But, I admired his conviction. His need to try, his need to make a statement against oppression, was just as obvious as the weight of that statue. Later in the day, I noticed that a crane had been brought in. The statue was face-down on the ground, Dzerzhinsky's stone face kissing the littered ground. I looked up and saw a group of KGB employees standing on the rooftop, quietly watching what was going on below them. It seemed as though they already knew about the events; maybe they had even orchestrated them. But, that was just my impression at the moment.

By the time the Soviet Union officially collapsed, I had received an invitation from the Foreign Minister of Azerbaijan. I left Moscow and became the Second Secretary of the Azerbaijani Foreign Ministry. I was responsible for relations with the U.S. and Canada. In 1992, I became one of the first diplomats in the Foreign Ministry of Independent Azerbaijan. My education and experience was quickly appreciated, and soon I was promoted to First Secretary.

That same year, I had my first combat experience. Since I was in charge of the Foreign Ministry's press service, I was asked to accompany a group of Western journalists to the war zone of the ongoing Azerbaijani-Armenian conflict over the Nagorno-Karabakh region. Those troubles actually started on the eve of the breakup of the USSR. At the time of my assignment in the Foreign Ministry, a part of the Azerbaijani territory had already been occupied by the Armenian forces and the fighting was still going on. Helicopters flew us from the capital, Baku, to the area of conflict in the Aghdam region of Azerbaijan. When we arrived, we picked up local residents and Azerbaijani soldiers, all of whom were badly wounded and needed to be taken to hospitals in Baku. When we arrived at the mobile train hospital, the smell of sweat and blood was overwhelming. Practically every bed and chair was being occupied by residents who had been caught in the middle of the fighting. The injuries ranged from badly scraped legs and forehead gashes to lost limbs and fatal gunshot wounds. No one was exempt from the fate of living in amidst a war; I watched an elderly woman and a young child took their final breaths inside that dilapidated train.

Surprisingly, the hospital was very close to the Armenian shelling positions, and it was obvious that it could be hit at any time. When we asked one of the Commanders about the logic of its location, he shrugged it off and scuttled away before giving us a specific answer. As though the sights of the hospital were not disturbing enough, we then went to a former warehouse that had been converted to a holding space for dead bodies. It was full of corpses. They were laid out side-by-side and head-to-foot, like bricks in a road. The bricks that build a war.

The correspondents were eager to take pictures and record everything that they saw. They said that they wanted to get closer to the Armenian positions, which were in the nearby village of Nakhichevanik. There were the main Armenian positions there from which they were preparing to advance. It was a very high-risk area; the shelling was virtually non-stop. We tried to explain to the correspondents that it would be very dangerous to get closer to the Armenian positions, but they did not want to listen. Finally, they began to move toward the shelling points. I had been instructed to accompany them everywhere, so I had to go with them.

We were getting closer and closer, and at one point the bullets started to fly above our heads. We had to keep down all the time. Fortunately, the correspondents came to realize the seriousness of the situation. Finally, when we were close enough to the Armenians, they realized that it had become too dangerous, and they decided to come back. We returned to Baku at the end of the day. My first combat mission was successful, though it has haunted me for years. For some time after that, my dreams consisted of the old woman's face and the sight of the bodies in the village warehouse. They are impossible to escape. I did not know then that many years would pass and I would go to war again. It would be a different war in a different country, but it would be built upon the same foundation of human suffering and tragedy.

It does not surprise me when I think about the global way in which my career has continued to unfold. In 1993, I became one of the first diplomats from Independent Azerbaijan to be sent to the embassy in Washington, D.C., which had recently been officially announced. I could feel history unfolding as we arrived in the U.S. and formally opened our embassy in the Mayflower Hotel.

Despite my busy schedule, education remained a top priority for me. In 1994 and 1995, trying to further develop my professional skills, I attended the International Public Policy Program for Mid-Career Professionals at Johns Hopkins University. Also in 1994, I attended the Special Course in Public Diplomacy, which was a joint program between the Institute of World Politics and Boston University. After my Soviet education, it was a unique opportunity to study in the U.S. The following year, I completed my diplomatic mission in the U.S. and came back to the Azerbaijani Foreign Ministry.

In 1996, in the wake of expanding relationships between

Azerbaijan and the West (especially the U.S.), I was offered and accepted a position as Vice President of the newly-established American University of Azerbaijan. My responsibilities involved coordination of the University's relations with U.S. institutions and research centers. As a logical continuation of those activities, I became a representative of the University and the president of the Azerbaijani-American educational center in Washington, D.C.

Living and working in the U.S. was a bright new chapter in my life. I found myself enjoying the country more and more with each new day. I was gaining more and more expertise later, working as a consultant for American multinational companies and then teaching foreign languages in the language institutes and the American University in Washington, D.C., as a visiting professor. Finally, I taught foreign languages and cultures in the Foreign Service Institute of the State Department before my deployment in Iraq with the U.S. Army. To me it was a logical continuation of my extensive and unusual background, which extended through the former USSR, independent Azerbaijan and the U.S. From each of those countries I received relevant educational, work and life experiences. Enriched with my combat experience in Iraq with the U.S. military, I felt a great degree of moral satisfaction with having lived an interesting and useful life. This satisfaction was increased when I came back to my family and my job at the State Department. I realized that my family was very much dedicated to me and my supervisors highly appreciated my service to the country. Still, I felt that I had a lot of energy and passion to accomplish more on the road ahead. I had this feeling the whole year I was in Iraq. I still have an impression that the next stage of my experience is going to be even more interesting, exciting and meaningful.

Chapter 7

The Problem of Insurgency and Terrorism

First of all, we need to define what "insurgency" is and what "terrorism" is. Are they the same? The DOD defines the term as "an organized movement aimed at the overthrow of a constituted government through use of subversion and armed conflict." (Al Qaeda as an insurgency. Joint Force Quarterly, Oct. 2005, by Michael F. Morris). According to the United Nations General Assembly cited by Wikipedia terrorism is "Criminal acts intended or calculated to provoke a state of terror in the general public, a group of persons or particular persons for political purposes are in any circumstance unjustifiable, whatever the considerations of a political, philosophical, ideological, racial, ethnic, religious or any other nature that may be invoked to justify them."

There were mostly three kinds of terrorist and insurgency groups operating in Iraq then: supporters of the former Baath regime of Saddam Hussein, local insurgents representing different competing groups, and "international fighters" coming mainly from Syria, Iran and other Arab and Muslim countries. The Islamic concept "Umma", which refers to the Islamic brotherhood without borders, seemed to be having a practical implication in Iraq. According to the interpretation of that definition, if your Muslim brother is in danger, no matter where you are you need to come and help him. As we know, Islam can be very broadly and flexibly interpreted, and it can be used for different political purposes. In some cases when Islam is being deliberately exploited by some leaders for their political purposes, others can sincerely believe in religious principles and choose to fight to achieve them. This last case is more dangerous and difficult to defeat, because in certain historical circumstances it can attract many followers locally and internationally as well. A clear example of the latter case was the late Ayatollah Ruhalla Khomeini, the highest Shiite spiritual leader in the 1970s. From his exile in Paris, he directed the Iranian Islamic revolution which led to the defeat of the government of the pro-Western Iranian Shah, the late Resa Pekhlevi. As in the case of Iran, where the followers of the Islamic revolution saw Western-style democracy as a real danger to their identity and culture, Islam has become a shield and ideology of protection against this factor among many groups and organizations operating in Iraq. This Islamic ideology is mainly typical of the last two groups mentioned, while the group, which mainly consists of the former members of the Baath party, is more nationalistic and secular, and their struggle is mainly aimed at regaining their lost political power and influence. The main purpose of these organizations is to achieve the withdrawal of all foreign forces, mainly American–the leading power in Iraq–because they regard those forces as a "foreign invasion of their lands" and a "conspiracy of great powers." The kidnappings, mortar and rocket attacks, car explosions, ambushes, etc., are carried out for that purpose. However, there are also many groups that are simply criminal in nature. They use kidnappings and other methods for commercial gain. They have nothing to do with the political or ideological struggle; rather, they found in these activities some kind of lucrative business for their personal enrichment. Sometimes they use the names of known terrorist organizations as a cover.

The following are the main insurgent groups which were or still operating in Iraq:

Former Members of Saddam Hussein's Baath Party and His Loyalists

These groups are active either by supporting insurgents financially or directly filling the ranks of the Iraqi insurgency. Many of them are members of Saddam's Republican Army, and they have combat experience, especially those who participated in the Iran-Iraq war. There was a lot of discussion at the time that Paul Bremer–former U.S. head of the transitional administration in Iraq–had made a mistake when he rushed to disband the Iraqi army in 2003, but he did not actually disarm it. As a result, loyalists of the former regime, unhappy with losing their power and privileges, joined the ranks of the Iraqi insurgency and brought weapons with them. This group is mainly secular and nationalistic, and it is predominately led by Saddam's former army commanders or his relatives, such as a nephew of the former leader, who was later captured and convicted by the Iraqi national court. Islam also is used by them as an ideology against the U.S. and coalition forces and as a way to recruit new members. The group is mainly active in central Iraq, in cities such as Fallujah, where there is a strong tradition of military service and respect for the former Iraqi military. It is believed that this group was at the forefront of the Iraqi insurgency. The group formed the core of the suppression of many of the radical Sunni, Shiite and Kurdish groups during the rule of Saddam Hussein.

"Al-Qaida in Iraq"

Formerly, the organization was known as "Tawhid and Jihad," Arabic for "Unity and the Holy War." It was led by Jordanian Abu-Musaib Az-Zarqawi until he was killed by a U.S. airstrike in 2006. He was replaced by Abu Ayyub Al-Misri (Egyptian) also known as Abu Ayyub Al-Muhajir (immigrant). He was also reportedly killed later.

These do not seem to be as numerous as the first group, but they are dedicated, sophisticated and highly visible and their actions are highly publicized. They are responsible for Iraq's bloodiest bombings and beheadings, including those of a number of Americans and British, such as U.S. citizen Nick Berg and British contractor Kenneth Bigley. According to U.S. and Iraqi government sources, Al-Qaida in Iraq is actively recruiting foreign fighters from countries such as Syria, Yemen, Sudan, Algeria, and Saudi Arabia. According to a report released in September 2005 by the Center for Strategic and

International Studies, the number of foreign insurgents in Iraq was about 10 per cent, which makes about three thousand fighters. The rest are Iraqi, mainly Sunni Arabs. A lot of financial support is being provided by Saudi fighters, and their deaths usually receive a higher profile in Arab media coverage. At the end of 2004, Abu-Musaib Az-Zarqawi renamed his organization "Al-Qaida in Iraq."

Zarqawi and his followers have long-standing combat experience from Afghanistan, where he was one of the commanders of a Jihadi training camp in the beginning of 2000. His followers are very mobile and decisive. They are well armed, but most importantly equipped with a highly motivating ideology of resistance to the "Western way of democracy," which they regard as a danger to their traditional way of life. They are highly suspicious of the coalition's actions in Iraq, regarding them as a plot hatched by the world's great powers to control their region and undermine their culture.

The main targets of this group in Iraq are U.S. and coalition forces and Iraq's slowly emerging security forces. The Kurdish community and the Shiite community are also targeted with the aim of igniting sectarian conflict. This last factor has lately become a central point in Zarqawi's strategy in Iraq. In their actions, the group is actively using the internet and television, such as the popular Arabic television network Al-Jazeera. Some of the organization's messages and their bloodiest beheadings were being widely broadcast, which gave the group a certain level of prominence and an image of capability.

"Ansar Al-Islam" (Arabic Supporters or Followers of Islam)

This group consists mainly of radical Sunni Kurds and also Arabs based in the mountainous parts of northern Iraq. It opposes Kurdish groups such as the Patriotic Union of Kurdistan, which is being supported by the U.S. At the beginning of the Iraqi war, the organization lost some of its bases as a result of U.S. bombings of that area. The group was particularly active through 2004, when it claimed responsibility for several suicide bomb attacks on the offices of the U.S.

backed political organizations, including Kurdish parties, and other actions, such as kidnappings and ambushes.

The leader of the organization is Mullah Krekar. According to the press, he is an ethnic Kurd and has lived in Norway as a refugee since 1991. The U.S. government believes that Ansar Al-Islam had ties with Osama Bin Laden's Al-Qaida organization, but it seems that, like many other Iraqi militant groups, this organization operates independently. Unlike, for example, "Al-Qaida in Iraq," this group does not seem to be trying to ignite sectarian tension by directing its activities against the Shiite community. Instead, they target anybody who is cooperating with the U.S. and coalition forces.

"The Mehdi Army"

The "Mehdi Army," is named after the twelfth Shiite Imam Mehdi who, according to the religious teaching, mystically disappeared, but is supposed to come back and secure the triumph of the Shiite religion among the Muslims. The leader of the "Army" is the young Shiite radical cleric Muqtada As-Sadr, who is a son of the late Ayatollah Muhamed As-Sadr, who was killed by Saddam's security forces. The supporters of this group are mainly from the Southern part of the country, which is predominately Shiite, and from the Shiite neighborhoods of Baghdad, particularly from Sadr City, which is named after Muqtada As-Sadr's father.

Like many other active Shiite clerics, Muqtada As-Sadr has been in exile in Iran and, after the fall of Saddam Hussein's regime, became very active both politically and militarily. His followers publish a newspaper reflecting the group's interests. The U.S. ban on the newspaper sparked sporadic clashes between As-Sadr's followers and U.S. troops since April 2004, and these clashes spread over to other Shiite areas across Iraq. That situation caused serious concern for the U.S., coalition forces and the Iraqi government, which at the time feared that further violence could get out of control.

The clashes erupted again in the summer of 2004, mainly in and around the holy city of Najaf. Only after the intervention and mediation of the top Iraqi Shiite cleric Ayatollah Ali As-Sistani the clashes were halted, and the "Mehdi Army" fighters who were taking cover inside of the Imam Ali shrine turned it over to the representatives of Ali Sistani.

The position of Muqtada As-Sadr toward the Iraqi government changes from time to time. At some points he supports it, at other points he opposes it.

Although As-Sadr and his followers, as well as other Shiite clerics, at times were critical of what they regarded as Ali Sistani's too moderate views, it is believed that Ali Sistani's influence has been crucial to keeping the Shiite community more predictable and controllable. It seems that now Shiite and Kurdish communities, after the long suppression by Saddam Hussein's minority Sunni, but secular, government, finally have a chance to prevail. It probably doesn't make much sense at this point for them to fight the coalition forces. Instead, they can take advantage of their presence, at least against the stubborn insurgency, which is predominately led by Sunni or Saddam loyalists. This might mean that the Shiite leadership and other major players in the country are following their political interests at this stage. Apparently, that is the main reason that none of the Shiite political figures are strongly demanding the withdrawal of the coalition forces yet. That might be the main argument As-Sistani used to restrain young Shiite charismatic clerics such as Muqtada As-Sadr, who is believed to have support from Iran and the Iran-backed Hezbollah in Lebanon. He was in Iran getting his clerical education from renowned Shiite authorities to become Marja'a Taqleed, which is the highest authority in Shiite clerical hierarchy. The apparent goal is to gain higher political clout and influence in the future political and religious life of Iraq. Reportedly he returned to Iraq on January 5, 2011. As-Sadr's return caps another dramatic rise to prominence for him and his followers after being routed by Iraqi and U.S. forces and appearing to fade from power just a few years ago. The strong showing by his bloc in last year's parliamentary elections and his key support for Prime-Minister Nouri al-Maliki paved the way for Wednesday's return. (*By QASSIM ABDUL-ZAHRA, Associated Press, Jan 5, 2011*)

After the political and security situation becomes stable, we might expect increasing demands by the Shiite Iraqi leadership to withdraw foreign troops from the country. Would the Shiite dominated government and Iraqi national parliament still be friendly toward the coalition and the U.S. at that point? It has to be seen.

"Mujahidin Shura Council"

In January 2006, an umbrella group reportedly was set up by Al-Qaida in Iraq (formerly the "Tawhid and Jihad" organization led by Abu Musaib Az-Zarqawi). In addition to Al-Qaida in Iraq, the Council includes such groups as: Jaish At-Taifa Al-Mansura, Ansar At-Tawhid, Al-Ghuraba, Al-Jihad Al- Islami and Al-Ahwal.

Those are the main anti-U.S., coalition and Iraqi government insurgent organizations and groups. Throughout the book, however, we will mention other groups that have been active in the Middle East for years and are now reemerging in Iraq.

The main features of such groups are that they are not coordinated from a single center. They are different in their tactics and strategy. Some of them are trying to achieve a Sunni Muslim caliphate similar to the one that existed centuries ago in the Muslim world. Others are fighting for a Shiite Islamic state like the one in Iran. It seems that some of the insurgency is dominated by the nationalistic sentiments and Islam is being used as an excuse for this struggle. This faction consists of former members of Saddam Hussein's Baath party and former commanders and members of his military.

There are different factors and incentives attracting new people to the ranks of the insurgency, including religious or nationalistic principles, lost privileges and income, and loss of loved ones during the Iraqi war.

According to various estimates, the numbers of active insurgents ranged from 30,000 to 200,000. It is believed that the number of foreign fighters was much fewer–probably several thousand–but they are usually more aggressive, and their attacks more deadly.

It is interesting to note that American and British officials have reported that weapons have been supplied to all of the insurgency groups in Iraq by both Syria and Iran. This would mean that Shiite Iran was supplying weapons to Sunni insurgents to kill Iraqi Shiites at the time.

In addition to those insurgent groups, there are other armed organizations, such as the Shiite Badr fighters mainly in the south and the Kurdish peshmerga, which controls the Kurdish northern areas, but they support the efforts of the coalition and the Iraqi government.

Chapter 8

Western Stimuli, the Rise of Militant Islam, and its Implications for Iraq and the Region

To understand the increased role of the "Islamic factor" in Iraq and elsewhere, we need to make a quick historical tour and analysis of its role in international relations. This "factor" has attracted the attention of American and Western experts of contemporary Islam. Islam has become a significant political phenomenon, not only in the internal political and social life of traditionally Islamic countries since the 1950s, but in international relations as well. The "Islamic Revivalism" of the 1970s and 1980s mainly consisted of three components: Islamic revolution in Iran, events in and around Afghanistan, and activation of the Muslim organizations and movements around the world. That period also witnessed the first signs of unification of some anti-Western regimes in the Middle East. These events have significantly changed the character of international relationships between the traditionally Muslim world and the West.

The West had to deal with a group of countries in which foreign policy was coordinated and integrated on a religious basis. Moreover, they had their international organizations partially or entirely based on the religious principals, such as: OIC (Organization of Islamic conference), LAC (The League of Arab Countries), RUD (The Regional Union of Development), OAPEC, OPEC, (regional oil exp. org.) IBD (Islamic Bank of Development and others).

According to the traditional perception of the "Islamic factor" by US and Western experts of Islam the technological and social progress would have inevitably led to the replacement of the religious views by the secular ones (Binder L., Ideological Revolution in the Middle East, N-4, 1964, p.p. 62-64.) In general, they ultimately expected to prevail of secularization in the traditionally Muslim societies.

The reality has refuted such an approach and compelled the Western researchers of Islam to acknowledge the erroneousness of that policy.

The American expert N. Keddi says that they (Western scholars) couldn't foresee and expect such a "strong attack" of the "Islamic Revivalism" in the late 1970s (Keddi N. Iran: Change in Islam. Islam and Change-International Journal of Middle East Studies, 1980, vol. 12, N.4, p.528.).

They also realized that the emergence of Colonel Muammar Kaddafi in Libya with his " third world theory" and Islamic Revolution in Iran were not the coincidence of circumstances but a result of the natural historical process. The essence of that process consisted of the appropriate psychological, socio-political and economic structure of world outlook which was taking shape during the centuries in this geopolitical area. Islam has become an integral part of this process as a "way of life". The Islamic ideology has actually adapted to these realities.

Thus Islam, traditional values, and culture merged together to make "Islamic civilization." So, religion as the ideological support of Islamic societies has always been a protector for people in different circumstances, in terms of their political, social, and economic lives, and especially in their relationships with other countries. Islam has always been some kind of banner and factor of consolidation of various stratums of society. For these countries, Islam is morale, discipline, and legal order(3) (Keddi N., " Iran: Change in Islam, Islam and Change," in *International Journal of Middle East Studies*, 1980, vol. 12, N.4, p.529.)

The vitality and "revivalism" of Islam can be explained through the following factors: nationalism, the peculiarity of Islamic mentality, centuries-old cultural heritage and legacy, the politicization of Islam, the modernization of Islam, the activation of the Islamic factor in international relations, and the role of the Western cultural influence.

The first "post-colonial stage," when the representatives of big business circles dominated in power, has been characterized by a "passion" for the modernization of social structure and the stimulation of capitalist and quasi-socialist methods of economic management. Therefore, an "imitation" of Western political models and ideas of governance was taking place.

The second stage in the development of Islamic countries took place during the 1970s and was coined by Western experts as "Islamic Revivalism." This was a short period of time during which significant changes in the socio-economic and political life of Muslim countries took place. As a result "the Islamic factor" started to play a significant role in international politics.

From the 1940s to the 1960s, the traditionally Muslim countries—which just gained their political independence—inherited weak economic and ideological systems and were mainly characterized by a great degree of passivity. During this time, there was a search for optimal options of national development, in order for them to overcome the backwardness of their economies and the difficult legacy of their feudal and half-feudal relations. However, there were many difficulties and challenges along the way, particularly in the sphere of ideology.

Given the perception of Islam that has persisted throughout the end of the nineteenth century, it is obvious that the type of reform that Jamal Ad-Din Afghani, Muhammad Abduh, and their followers tried to enact could not fully adapt Islam to the requirements of the new realities. This particular circumstance did not allow the Islamic groups to formulate the concepts of social development during the long postcolonial period of time. This is why the Western and American models of economic, political and military development were attractive to the leading Muslim countries until the mid-1950s. But the process of developing the national ideology took place in the Islamic societies in the 1950s and 1960s in each of the Muslim countries in varying forms and different degrees of intensity. Islam was at the center of the modernization process. The Modernist Movement took place until the end of the 1960s. Modernists' efforts were aimed at revising the interpretations of the religious dogmas and conceptions, so as to adapt them to the demands of the present time. They hoped to combine the ideology of "Contemporary Islam" with the elements of traditionalism and reformism. Moreover, some of them believed that Islamic theory did not have the necessary ideological potential to provide for all spheres of the state, public, and family lives. In connection to this, there were strong tendencies in the official ideology of the Muslim countries to limit the use of Islam by the spheres of education, culture, and ethics. In opposition to the Modernists, there were the Traditionalists, who consolidated their efforts and leaned on the poor and unsatisfied stratums of the populations. They came out in defense of the preservation and expansion of Islamic theory in the Muslim countries, desiring it to be a dominant ideology. During the latter part of the 1970s, and during the course of this struggle between the Modernists and Traditionalists, a new political stage emerged: Islamic Revivalism. Islamic Revivalism was not only the result of the mentioned struggle, but mainly the result of significant changes that took place in the political, economic, social, and ideological spheres of the Muslim countries.

The supporters of Islamic Revivalism have been gradually taking the initiative. When the Islamic countries have completed the process of strengthening their national sovereignty and reached a certain level of socio-economic transformations, the qualitative change of the tendency began to take place in the policy of reforming Islam. This change was characterized by a weakening of the Modernists' influence in the political and philosophical lives of the Islamic societies, and an increase in the demand of some kind of different, alternative, and more national ideology based on Islam and diametrically opposed to the democratic capitalist system and the Western conception of freedom and liberalism.

There are four main schools of Sunni Islam: Hanbali, Hanafi, Shafi'i, and Maliki. Together, they comprise a significant majority of Muslims. Beyond that, the Salafi (Arabic for "predecessors") movement, under the leadership of Syrian Rashid Rida (1865-1935) followed the activities of Muhammad Abduh and steadily moved towards the type of fundamentalism that later prevailed after the failure of Modernization and Westernization in the Muslim Societies. The Wahhabi sect, named after the 18th-century thinker Muhammad Ibn Abd al-Wahhab and inspired by 13th-century Syrian theologian Ibn Taymiya, is part of the broader Salafi movement. The Salafi movement rejects many mainstream "innovative" Islamic traditions in favor of a "pure" Islam. Organizations such as Hizb at-Tahrir (The Party of Liberation), Al-Qaida (the raising base), Hamaas (enthusiasm), Islamic Jihad (the Holy War), and Ikhwan Muslimin (Muslim Brotherhood) share the same kind of ideology with different political agendas.

The failure of the Western Movement, the withdrawal of the Soviets from Afghanistan and subsequent demise of the Soviet Union, as well as the above factors, created a favorable ground for the next stage in Islamic Revivalism. This time, it was aimed against Western democracy, liberalism, freedom, initiative, and individualism. The culmination of that stage was September 11, 2001.

An additional factor influencing anti-Western sentiments in Muslim communities is the collective influence of the outdated legal and security mechanisms that do not allow them to effectively operate against the radicals in Europe and other societies, where they openly regard liberal democracy as "*haram*," or "forbidden by God."

Now, Europe is beginning to realize the dangers of alienating its Muslim population. Because of insufficient immigration systems and the lack of meaningful and active roles for Muslim residents in the economic, social, and political lives of their respective countries of residence, they are becoming a favorable ground for radical recruitment. Multiculturalism of the European societies would be an effective mechanism to prevent the radicalization of the Islamic community.

Ironically, the situations in Iraq, Afghanistan, Chechnya and

Bosnia were helping the radical Islamist groups to recruit new members. They justified this as a "war against Muslims."

It is becoming increasingly clear that the only way for the West to prevent the spread of militant Islam is to win the hearts and minds of Muslims. Muslims should become equal members of the Multicultural Western societies. In that case, "Western Conspiracy" against the Muslim societies would lose its ground.

The point about alienation is clearly seen when looking at Turkey, which is an important ally and the only Muslim member of NATO. It is also strategically located next to Iraq and other Muslim countries, including Iran, Afghanistan and the Muslim republics of the former USSR. The failure to accept Turkey to the European Union could further alienate the country and create a favorable atmosphere for radical Islamic trends. The radicals can explore the concept of "Christian West Conspiracy" against "Muslim Turkey." In fact, anti-Western and anti-American sentiments in Turkey are currently at a record high.

The traditionally Muslim republics of the former USSR, such as Uzbekistan, Tajikistan, Kirgizstan, and Azerbaijan are also going to be very important for the global geopolitics during the next decades to come. The recent bloody revolt and regime change in Kirgizstan, a small former Soviet Central Asian Republic, which hosts the major U.S. air base "Manas" for military operations in Afghanistan caused a lot of concern among U.S. officials. Statements of some leaders of the new interim government indicated that the lease could not be extended after its expiration.(4). *Stephanie Gaskell, Daily News, April 8, 2010.*

The previous passage is an example of how the wrong message and a lack of relevant engagement on the part of the West could create the same kind of challenges in that part of the world which the West is presently facing in the Middle East.

The war on terrorism and insurgency emphasizes the importance of cultural awareness.

We need to keep in mind the simple cultural differences between the traditionally Muslim countries and the West. For example, Arab societies have a different attitude towards work; the typical American habit of "keeping busy" is an alien concept for the majority of Muslim societies.

Gulf oil rich Arab countries are spending a tremendous amount of resources to hire foreigners to do their work for them, instead of investing in their economy and education. To a certain extent, that explains why Muslim societies have been left behind in their economic and technological development.

In turn, it deepens the traditional perception that all the troubles come from the "Christian West," with its "conspiracy theories:" the traditional Arab concept of "you" and "us."

Among other challenges that the West will have to face include the fact that many Arab and non-Arab Muslims see the current wave of terrorism as a clash of civilizations and some actions of the West in the Middle East and elsewhere as a "hidden agenda" and a "conspiracy" against their cultural and historical identity. This notion is widespread on the grassroots level in Iraq, Afghanistan, and other predominantly Muslim countries. The military presence of the Western countries in the region strengthens that belief. Muslims frequently refer to what they feel is the West's one-sided support of Israel. Al-Qaida and leaders of other terrorist and insurgency organizations accuse the U.S. of supporting dictatorships in Arab countries such as Saudi Arabia and Jordan, and they use this notion as another recruitment tool. Finally, the flexibility of Islam and the Koran gives different Muslim leaders and politicians the opportunity to interpret various aspects of international politics and social life in accordance with their political agendas.

The present war with terror and insurgency is multi-polar.

We are dealing with diverse targets with different cultures, political agendas, and strategies. The Cold War, bipolar approach was effective against the Soviet Union and the Warsaw pact because it was a single ideological entity. The same approach in the current war on terrorism would make many Muslims believe that the West—the U.S., in particular—is engaged in a war against Islam.

Many radicals and some Muslims see Western democracy based on the so-called "new liberalism," freedom, initiative, and opportunity at the individual level as a threat to their cultural values and identity.

We need to be clear and specific on how we define our language.

This is the war against violent extremism, regardless of a particular religion. This is not a war against terrorism (too vague) or Islam as a whole.

It is important to possess knowledge on the history, cultural nuances, and customs of the targeted audience if we want to win their hearts and minds. For that goal, we need to actively engage the local population, analyze its behavior, isolate the radicals, and avoid alienating the majority of Muslims, because they are potential allies.

It is important to know and understand the actions of the enemy, their political agendas, their strategic goals, and their social support (Sun Tzu).

Planning and conducting effective strategic communication measures using all of the above factors and utilizing all available technologies are vital for the success of the mission. Finally, it is also crucial that there are sufficient immigration systems and that Muslim residents are active in the economic, social, and political lives of their countries of residence.

Chapter 9

The Religious and Ethnic Diversity of Iraq

Iraq was known for centuries as Mesopotamia. The country was the home of the Sumerians, the Babylonians, the Assyrians and the Arabs. In the sixteenth century, Iraq became part of the Turkish Ottoman Empire until its collapse after World War One. After the war, the lands of the Ottoman Empire were divided among the victorious allies, according to the peace agreement. Some of the territory under British control became the independent country of Iraq. This lasted until 1958 when a group of army officers killed the British appointed king and declared Iraq to be a republic.

The majority of the approximately 28 million Iraqi people, about 60 percent, belong to the Shiite branch of the Islamic religion. The rest are members of another branch of Islam: Sunnism.

In addition to Shiite and Sunni Arabs, the majority of the Iraqi Kurds are Sunni. There are also Esidi Kurds and a relatively small number of Shiite Kurds. There is also a small community of Christians.

The Sunni Arabs are mainly concentrated in the following parts of the country: the Baghdad area, western Anbar province, Tikrit and Mosul.

The Kurdish population is mainly in the North, with Sunni Kurds in the city of Irbil and other areas, and with Esidi Kurds near the cities of Mosul and Dohuk. There is also a small Bedouin population in the desert areas.

In Kirkuk is the area of the Turkoman population and an important oil pipeline stretches through this area.

Shiites predominate in the South, with their religious centers in the holy cities of Najaf and Karbala. There is a mosque in Najaf where Imam Ali, the founder of Shiite Islam is buried. (After the death of the prophet Mohamed, fighting ensued over who would become the ruling Caliph. As a result of that struggle, the second branch of Islam, Shiism emerged).

The Caliphate was an Islamic state where the head of state and the religious leader was the same person. It gradually expanded into a vast territory in the Middle East, Africa and Europe. Islam was accepted by many countries as a result of the expansionist wars of the Caliphate rulers. It was also accepted voluntarily as a convenient ideology for local leaders to control and run their countries.

Saddam Hussein's government, although secular, represented the Sunni minority and many Shiite leaders were executed by the regime. The father of Muqtada As-Sadr was one of those leaders executed by Hussein's regime.

Some Shiites, including Muqtada As-Sadr himself, were in exile during the years of Saddam Hussein's regime, mainly in neighboring Iran. They had good links and relations with the Iranian ruling clerics all those years and naturally there is a significant influence of Iran on their views about the issues of Islam, politics and statehood, etc. After the ousting of Saddam Hussein, the majority of them returned to Iraq. Fortunately, another Iraqi exile in Iran, the most respected and top Shiite leader Grand Ayatollah Ali As-Sistani, seems to have moderate views. So far he has not opposed the coalition forces deployed in the country. Moreover, he has been very supportive of the positive political processes going on in the country. His influence among the majority Shiites was and still is crucial for maintaining relative stability and security. There is little doubt, however, that he has been influencing the political life of the country through his Fatwas (religious directives) while officially maintaining his noninterference in politics. In our opinion this tactic might be used to retain a Shiite power which also boosts the Iranian influence in Iraq and the region.

Spoken languages in Iraq include Arabic, Kurdish, Turkoman, Assyrian and others.

Iraq is the only Arab country where the majority of the population follows the Shiite branch of Islam. The rest of the Arab world is predominantly Sunni. Iran also is majority Shiite but ethnically the Iranians are Persians, not Arabs.

While in Iraq, I had the interesting experience of observing differences between these two main Iraqi religious communities: the Shiites and the Sunnis.

Besides the differences in their religious teachings, under Saddam Hussein's government, Iraqi Sunnis had been given more opportunities for education. As a result, their literacy level is much higher than that of the Iraqi Shiites and their economic conditions were also better. The Shiite community was subjected to repression by Saddam's government, which also lowered their living standards.

While in Iraq, I went on military missions to the villages in the central area of the country, where the population is largely mixed; Sunnis live alongside Shiites. Looking at the houses, though, you could easily see which house was Shiite and which was Sunni. Usually on the roof of a Sunni house you could see one flag colored green, which is the color of Islam. On the top of a Shiite house, however, there were usually three flags: green, black and red. Green is the color of the religion, black denotes mourning for their Imams (Ali, Hussein, and others) killed centuries ago, and red signifies revenge against those who killed the Imams.

In terms of clothing, for example, the traditional Arab men's headscarf, called "shumaakh," or "shmaakh" (in Iraqi dialect) is also different for each group. Sunnis usually wear a "shumaakh" with red and white squares on it. The Shiites' "shumaakh" is black and white. Generally, black seems to be a popular and traditional color among Shiites. It symbolizes mourning and sadness, particularly for the murdered Imams and other loved ones. But we believe that the color of the shumaakh is not a clear indicator of a Sunni or Shiite. Red and White are typically worn by men from a country with a monarch. (Saudi Arabia, Jordan). Black (or Grey) and White is worn by men from a country under Presidential rule (Libya, Egypt). If they have not yet made the Hajj, the pilgrimage to Mekka, they wear a pure white shumaakh.

This religious and ethnic diversity has existed throughout history. Some of the differences were artificially created by the external powers, mainly the Ottoman Empire and British, who sought to control the region easier through igniting ethnic and religious animosity rather than unity. Throughout the history of Iraq this diversity and animosity between the religious and ethnic groups have fostered a potential instability in the country. This factor is also one of the main impediments to stabilizing the security situation and developing democracy in the country. Some insurgency groups tried to ignite the ethnic and religious tensions in Iraq for their own political agendas. The greatest concern in 2004-2006 was that those tensions could lead to a civil war that would be major disaster for the U.S., coalition and Iraqi government, as well as for the entire country and the region as a whole.

Chapter 10

The Security Situation and Mistakes of Coalition Forces

The general security situation remained unpredictable and uncertain, and there was a concern that it could explode at any time. Mistakes were made by the American troops, mainly because of a lack of knowledge of the region. According to Raed and Sami—two local Iraqi translators—the Abu Ghraib prison incident was one of the most significant blows to American-Iraqi cooperation and to the international prestige of the United States. A few American soldiers in that prison, which is located in the Baghdad area, abused Iraqi prisoners "just for fun." This incident received international media coverage and led to immense pressure on the U.S. administration and the U.S. military. A criminal investigation was underway before the publicity, but that was ignored by the international media. Some American soldiers were court-martialed and sentenced to prison; the media did not report this fact, out of fear that it would harm the reputation of the United States. This single incident inflicted substantial damage to the image of the U.S. during that important and difficult historical period.

Another notable event was the public pre-trial of former Iraqi President Saddam Hussein which, in the opinion of many observers and local Iraqis, was a mistake. This public event, and the way it was conducted, was perceived by many Iraqis, particularly Sunnis, as an insult to them, because Saddam was still their former President, and the appointed prosecutor in the case was a young man who, according to the Iraqi and Arab customs was unacceptable; According to their logic, the prosecutor should have been aged, gray-haired and a known and respected person. This event also sparked significant demonstrations, mainly in the Sunni-dominated central regions of the country.

During that period the security situation was deteriorating and tragic incidents were happening constantly.

In July of 2004, four Turkish truck drivers, whose vehicles were part of a U.S. military convoy, were ambushed and attacked by Iraqi insurgents. I was asked to come over to the military hospital to assist in communicating with them. One truck driver was critically wounded and his life was still in danger at the time. His brother, who was also a victim, was slightly injured, as was a third man. The fourth was shot in both legs and his condition was still critical. He was expected to have surgery the next morning. One of the slightly wounded truck drivers was a brother of the first seriously injured one, and he was emotional in expressing his concern, crying and begging to help his brother. My first impression, though, was that the doctors were still unsure whether or not the patient was going to survive.

I visited the wounded contractors again the next day after they had their surgery, and I was told by the doctors that the wounded driver who had been in the most critical condition would probably survive. Having heard the news, his brother was very happy and, with tears in his eyes, he was telling us again and again in a broken English, "Thank you, thank you…" It really was an emotional and touching scene.

Also, in July 2004, we went with the Civil Affairs Unit on our next mission to the local village to provide medical assistance. I was part of a dental group providing interpretation and communication support between our military medics and the Iraqis. I enjoyed that particular mission very much, because it gave us an opportunity to feel the Iraqi cultural spirit. During our entire mission, we could tell that they were very grateful to us.

I honestly believe that these activities establish bridges between the Iraqi and American forces, reducing the political and cultural differences between them. Unfortunately, those differences—particularly the cultural gap existing between the Americans and Iraqis—could be seen very clearly on many occasions. The main reason for it was often lack of understanding by some soldiers of the local Iraqi culture and customs.

According to Raed, the local Arabic translator for the Civil Affairs Unit, there were two main stages in the American and Coalition military operation in Iraq. The first period was very successfully completed; the majority of the Iraqi people were happy to get rid of the oppressive Saddam Hussein regime and greeted the Coalition forces. Real problems emerged after that, however, at the second stage of the mission, because the Americans didn't know how to deal with Iraqis. Raed believed that this psychological and cultural gap was still growing.

As an example, Raed mentioned an incident that occurred during a joint patrol mission that was comprised of four American soldiers and one Iraqi recruit, who had been trained by the Americans. They went to one of the villages, checking for insurgents' hideouts. At one of the houses, the Iraqi soldier told his American colleagues that he couldn't go inside of that particular house; his cousin who lived there would recognize him, and his life and the lives of his family would be in danger. The American soldiers insisted that the Iraqi recruit had to go first. One of the Americans got angry and punched the Iraqi so hard that he started to bleed. According to Raed, it is a very serious insult for the Iraqis to be treated like that. As a result, the Iraqi soldier pulled up his AK-47 rifle, shooting all four American soldiers and fleeing the scene. In Raed's opinion, it was a clear example of the cultural misunderstanding between the sides.

In July 2004, a mortar grenade attack occurred at the contractors' trailer on the base. As a result, 35 employees were wounded and one female contractor remained in critical condition. Subsequently, this particular incident led to the resignation of many contractors. On another day in July 2004, I had just left the shower trailer when I heard a blast somewhere nearby, behind the row of trailers. At first, I thought it was outgoing fire by our soldiers, but at that moment a group of

Filipino contractors rushed toward me, shouting, "Sir, look, look!" I looked in their direction and saw dust and smoke rising up. I realized that a mortar round had just landed close to us. The Filipinos were scared and didn't know what to do. I told them to get under cover at a nearby concrete bunker or hardened building, in case a second round of attack would occur. I waited until they went to the nearby bunker.

Later, I was told that the mortar ordnance landed two hundred yards from us. We were lucky that the shrapnel either went in different directions or the mortar was not a very large one. Otherwise, the deadly metal pieces of the explosion could have reached us.

On July 17, 2004, the day of my birthday, I left Iraq to go back home for a two-week vacation. The main purpose of my trip back to the United States was to be interviewed for my U.S. citizenship. That interview was scheduled for July 21. After waiting at the military base's airport practically all night, I was flown to the Rhein Main U.S. military base in Frankfurt, Germany. On July 19, I took a civilian Lufthansa Airline plane to Dulles International Airport. When I left customs, my wife and daughter rushed toward me, kissing and hugging me with tears in their eyes. Over the next several days, I enjoyed spending all my time with them.

Chapter 11

Trying to Become a New American

On July 21, I went to the interview, excited that soon I would become a U.S. citizen. But this turned out to be a complete disappointment when I had to deal with the bureaucratic environment of this agency. I passed the interview, answered all the questions and then the representative told me that there is another stage: the swearing in. He said that it was going to be a separate process but nobody knew when that would take place. I tried to explain that I had to go back to Iraq and I would like to complete the procedure while I was in the States because it was very difficult to come back again from Iraq any time soon. I also tried to show him the very supportive letters that were given to me by my military commanders in Iraq in appreciation of my work. I soon realized, though, that neither the representative of the immigration agency nor his supervisor really cared about such things. They didn't even look at the letters or make a copy of them to attach to the file. The supervisor told me that even if I came in a military uniform, it wouldn't have helped. I left in a very sad mood, completely upset after going through that unpleasant experience. I guess all the bureaucracies in the world are the same; they are always negative. I felt that nobody cared about my situation. It was especially upsetting because I went to Iraq to be of help to my new country.

After failing to get my citizenship then, I took a plane on August 1, 2004, heading to Frankfurt, Germany. I arrived in Frankfurt on August 2, as scheduled. After waiting several days for a military plane, I finally arrived in Iraq. The everyday work started again. Everybody in my unit was asking about my U.S. citizenship situation, and I had to explain what happened. Two days later I saw Colonel Z., the commander of my unit. Having known the outcome of my citizenship request, he was also upset and he couldn't understand why it happened that way.

Chapter 12

Planning for a Long Stay

After arriving at the U.S. military air base "Anaconda", I saw many changes. The base kept growing and construction was expanding. At that point, I realized that we were going to stay in Iraq for a long time. Many soldiers looked increasingly tired, but the morale seemed to remain high. Nobody that I talked to thought that the outcome of the U.S. presidential elections in 2004 was going to significantly change the U.S. policy in Iraq and the broader Middle East.

Chapter 13

Looking for New Opportunities

On August 12 my employer's manager in Iraq told me that they might be able to promote me to an executive position in their headquarters in California, but only after I get my U.S. citizenship. He said that there could be many opportunities for me at that stage. He also mentioned the possibility of transferring me to the northern Iraq for a change. So I realized that my only option was to wait until I get my citizenship and, after the completion of my assignment in Iraq, to try to apply for an executive position with the Company or for one of the Federal government agencies which might need my professional skills.

Chapter 14

Dealing with the Worsening Security Situation

August 6. According to the U.S. military officials, a suicide attacker sped up to a U.S. military convoy outside Fallujah and killed seven U.S. marines and three Iraqi soldiers. It was one of the deadliest days for American forces in Iraq in the last four months. This attack brought the number of U.S. service members who have died in Iraq since the beginning of military operations in March 2003 to 990.

There are also reports of increasing numbers of anti-American fighters being recruited in different Arab and Muslim countries by various Islamist organizations. The recruits are predominantly teenagers and they are being sent to Iraq through Syria, Saudi Arabia, Iran, Kuwait, and Jordan. It is believed that the governments of Iran and Syria are involved.

In Pakistan on the eve of the September 11th anniversary, anti-American and anti-Coalition demonstrations are being prepared by the Islamist groups, which opposed the war in Iraq.

On August 13, the Arabic and Turkish signs that I made for my military Unit in Iraq were finally shipped back from the States. They were nicely designed in white and blue on big metal sheets. They were placed in various areas around the base. This would leave a good memory of my work here in Iraq for many years to come. I was very pleased to see the final product of my work, which took me some time to complete.

August 14. I am at work with a military trans unit (transportation unit) that sets up convoys that carry military and civilian cargo throughout Iraq. This is a very important task; as it provides logistical support for the entire theater of the U.S. military operations in the country.

After an insurgent attack, a Turkish truck driver contractor, who was part of the U.S. military convoy, left his badly damaged vehicle near the Iraqi city of Samarra. He asked for our help to recover the truck, but unfortunately, there was nothing we could do except to give him a letter to submit to his company, explaining what had happened to the truck. He brought pictures which proved that his truck was completely destroyed. He was very upset because of the incident and the loss of the vehicle.

August 16. We went on a mission to the local village with the Civil Affairs Unit for an opening ceremony of a new school. The village is located about fifty minutes from "Anaconda" air base. It has a mixed population of Shiite and Sunni Arabs, but predominantly Shiite Muslims. We took pictures with local villagers and had very useful contacts with them. They were telling us that they had been receiving threatening letters from the "bad guys" (insurgents) for some time. Colonel Z. promised to investigate the issue.

August 17. Today's meeting with the local police Chief was the continuation of those complaints. I was asked to translate this meeting, which was very interesting and constructive.

The Chief was asked to increase the security and improve the protection of the villagers. The Chief, however, was trying to make a point that compared to other regions of Iraq, his area was much more secure. After the meeting, I was taken to another unit that needed my help.

While driving to the second meeting, we had an interesting conversation with Lt. Col. I., who works with us in the Civil Affairs Unit. He particularly mentioned that the situation had become more unpredictable and dangerous beginning in February 2004, when insurgents and supporters of the defeated Saddam Hussein started to surface. I remembered that the police chief at the previous meeting also mentioned that the tense and dangerous situation existed in practically the entire country.

When I reached the yard for staging military convoys, I was told that two mortar grenades had hit the spot close to our military office not long ago. As a result of the attack four persons were wounded, but fortunately none of them were critically injured.

On August 18 and 19, we were continuing to fix the signs that I had designed before for the military convoy staging area. Then Capt. B. (the commander of the transunit), Capt. S. and I had a meeting with one of the contractor managers, who mentioned to us that out of 300 employees several months ago only four persons were left. According to him, all of them quit because of the security situation. Some of them didn't even get off the plane when they arrived in Iraq, asking to go back to the States.

Capt. B. said that April was one of the worst months in terms of the security situation, because of the incidents that increased significantly. Many truck drivers and accompanying military personnel were killed in different regions of Iraq in that period, including some in the Baghdad area's Green Zone, which houses the foreign embassies and government agencies.

The contractor mentioned one recent incident, which occurred when he was a part of the military convoy moving at night when, as a result of a roadside bomb explosion, two persons were injured. According to him, the bomb was set up by the insurgents' right before the convoy approached the spot. The door of one of the trucks was completely smashed, and the driver could have lost his leg.

In reply to the contractor, Capt. B. said that many contractors quit because they realized that, if they were dead or severely injured, they wouldn't be able to spend the money that they had earned. The contractor said that only the craziest people were left and continued to work in Iraq.

Capt. B. said that, unlike the civilian employees, the military reserve did not have any option other than to stay in Iraq for at least another year. Answering the question as to whether all those attacks and security incidents were preventable, Capt. B. said that the U.S. military had been quite passive, since the Iraqis now had their sovereignty. These incidents would have been prevented if the U.S. military had been more aggressive.

As **of August 20**, the situation in the South remains tense. Fighting between the American forces and the Iranian- influenced Mehdi Army under the leadership of the radical Shiite cleric Muqtada As-Sadr, is sporadically erupting in and around the holy Shiite city of Najaf and Baghdad's As-Sadr city. A delegation from the Iraqi National Council was sent to negotiate a peaceful settlement with As-Sadr's followers, asking them to give up the armed struggle and to join the political process as a political party. Despite some progress, however, the fighting around the shrine Al-Imam Ali continued from time to time.

The continuing violence in the predominately Shiite South has seriously undermined the credibility of the new Iraqi government in the eyes of the Iraqis. At the same time, the latest polls on American public opinion on the war in Iraq show the shift in American public sentiments.

They reflect the difficulties in Iraq, including a death toll of nearly 1,000 U.S. soldiers, the insurgency against the new Iraqi government and U.S. forces, and the failure to find weapons of mass destruction, which was one of the main reasons for the Bush administration's decision to go to war.

August 21. A contractor came in and asked me to translate materials related to the opening of a new Turkish school. Later, I went to the army's legal office to try to get help with the issue of my U.S. citizenship. I passed the interview on July 21, 2004, but, the date for the last stage, the swearing in, is not yet set.

As of August 21, the situation in Najaf, a predominately Shiite City, remained tense. Muqtada As-Sadr rejected an ultimatum of the Iraqi government which included a demand to disarm his Mehdi Army. Otherwise the government indicated that it would use military force to compel As-Sadr's militiamen to give up arms. As-Sadr was also supposed to sign a statement saying that he would refrain from future violence and release all civilians and Iraqi security forces who had been kidnapped. Also according to the statement, As-Sadr had to hold a news conference and publicly announce that he was disbanding the Mehdi Army. The Arab League chief Amr Moussa on Thursday expressed his concern about the situation in Najaf particularly on the "renewal of shelling and clashes".

On August 21 there was another mortar attack close to our work place. The situation is becoming more and more unpredictable. We don't know what is going to happen next. I think nobody knows. I was in the trailer office with Capt. S. and my military partner, when we heard a blast and vibration that shook the trailer. A mortar landed not very far from us.

August 22. Fighting between the militants loyal to Muqtada As-Sadr and U.S. forces continued around the sacred Imam Ali shrine compound, near the old city and Najaf's vast cemetery.

There was an earlier announcement by As-Sadr's representative about removing their weapons from the shrine, and turning the holy site over to representatives of Iraq's top Shiite cleric Grand Ayatollah Ali Al-Husseini As-Sistani. But the transfer bogged down Saturday amid arguments over the technicalities of its implementation. As-Sadr's office said that they were trying to give the keys of the sacred compound to representatives of As-Sistani, who refused to accept them. As-Sistani himself was undergoing medical treatment in London.

One expert's opinion is that the continuation of the violence in Najaf, which had already spread to other Shiite communities across Iraq, posed the greatest risk to the interim government of Prime Minister Ayad Allawi. The earlier intentions to raid the mosque could turn the nation's majority of Shiites against the government, particularly if U.S. forces were involved. The issue remained sensitive and challenging, and the entire security situation in Iraq has been shaken by the events in Najaf.

On August 23, I went to the legal office to check on my U.S. citizenship. They sent a message to the U.S. Immigration Services, requesting they expedite my swearing-in date. Capt. D. asked me to stop by on Friday; hopefully, he will have a reply by then. On the way to work I stopped by the medical office. They gave me pills for my dust allergy and the stomach problems that I have been experiencing.

When I got to the office, a Turkish and a Saudi truck driver came in. While on the way to our base as part of a military convoy, they had been hit by roadside bomb explosions set up by the insurgents. The Turkish driver managed to drive his truck to the base, but he was wounded near his ear. The Saudi contractor lost his truck, which was badly damaged by the explosive, and we gave him an incident report to fill out. He should be able to get compensation from his company. Unfortunately, he also left some of his documents inside of the vehicle. The two incidents occurred in Northern Iraq, one in the area of Bayji and the second near the large and restive city of Mosul, which is famous for the insurgent activities there. According to Capt. S., those kinds of incidents become more frequent recently.

At 6:10 a.m. on August 24, I was awakened by the sound of a mortar attack. This time, it took quite a while before the all—clear was sounded. I didn't wait for the all—clear and went out to take a shower. It is usually risky, because you never know when a second round of the attack might hit. Fortunately, everything went well and I went to work. The rest of the day passed without any incidents.

On August 25, I felt much better. I had been sick for the last several days with a dust allergy and stomach problems, which are common for our service members and contractors here in Iraq. Several Turkish contractors came into our office. Their truck broke down behind the south gate and they needed help bringing it back to the base. They were part of a U.S. military convoy that was heading to our base. Their truck was recovered the next day.

On August 27, I went to the legal office to inquire about my swearing-in date. My appointment was set up for 1:00 p.m., but Capt. P., whom I was supposed to meet, was not in the office.

We received information that the highest Ayatollah Ali As-Sistani, met with Muqtada As-Sadr. Apparently they reached an agreement, saying that supporters of As-Sadr should lay down their arms and leave the area of the Holy Imam Shrine. The fighting has died down today. Is it really a stable cease-fire? The future will show. Unfortunately, similar deals have been reached in the past, but they never lasted long.

August 29, It has been calm in Najaf since Saturday. Shiite militants and U.S. forces battled Saturday in As-Sadr. As a result, five people were killed and dozens were wounded. As-Sadr is a stronghold of As-Sadr's Mehdi Army militia. Another major development took place on Friday, when U.S. air strikes hit Fallujah's eastern Al-Askari neighborhood, as well as the industrial area of the city, which has long been a symbol of Sunni insurgency. According to medical officials, three people were killed in the air strikes and 13 were wounded, including a 6-year-old girl.

For the first time, President Bush has acknowledged that he miscalculated the postwar situation in Iraq, meaning particularly the Iraqi insurgency. The expectation was that the former Iraqi dictator's National Guard would stand and fight. Instead, it disappeared, went underground, and later reemerged as a part of the Iraqi insurgency.

On August 30, I went back to the office. Several soldiers were waiting for our military team. They needed information on the military convoys. Later in the day, a group of truck driver-contractors came in. They were subjected to a large scale attack from Iraqi insurgents about 20 kilometers from the base. As a result, one Turkish truck driver was killed and three trucks were left on the road. The rest of the convoy arrived at the base at about 1:00 a.m. The contractors prepared an incident report that would be presented to the companies for compensation.

On August 31, Efforts are made to extend the Najaf peace deal to Baghdad's Sadr city. For that purpose, U.S., British, and Iraqi government forces are negotiating with supporters of Muqtada As-Sadr.

In the meantime, an insurgency website showed 12 kidnapped Nepalese workers reading a statement warning workers against going to Iraq and blaming America for lying about the security situation in the country. The kidnappings have been announced by the group called Ansar As-Sunna Army, which has also claimed responsibility for previous kidnappings.

In a separate incident, two Turkish hostages—Ali Diskin and Abdullah Ozdemir—were reportedly freed by Iraqi militants on Sunday, after the hostages' employers said that they were ending operations in Iraq to save the lives of their employees. "They are now at the embassy in Baghdad," Turkish Foreign Ministry spokesman Namik Tan told the Associated Press. The militants had said they would kill the two men if their companies did not leave Iraq within several days. A few hours later, the two companies that employed the men said they were withdrawing all staff from Iraq.

In another incident, two French journalists, Christian Chesnot and Georges Malbrunot, were reportedly taken hostage by militants in Iraq, who demanded that France revoke its law banning Islamic head scarves in schools. It looks like the security situation is not improving at this time. Many contractors are complaining that they are constantly being attacked on the roads, even when they are part of U.S. military convoy. Sometimes, the local Iraqis throw stones at them. Those attacks usually happen when the attackers think that there is not going to be retaliation from the U.S. military. For example, when the military passes and the rest of the convoy is lagging behind.

At 8:00 p.m., Col. Z. and Maj. L. of the Civil Affairs Unit took me with them to a dinner arranged by the local Iraqi contractors. We arrived there by about 9:00 p.m. and met several other U.S. personnel who had also been invited to the dinner. I met Joanna of the U.S. Air Force, who was of Polish origin, and we spoke some Russian, which is in the same Slavic linguistic family as Polish. Ibrahim, the Iraqi engineer-contractor, introduced us to other Iraqi contractors, who were also engaged in different projects on the base. Ibrahim showed us some papers describing the scope of work his company does, and he expressed an interest in the future projects of our Civil Affairs Unit. I also met the Air Force interpreter Sami, who is an ethnic Turkoman from the Iraqi northern city of Kirkuk. He currently resides in the U.S., but grew up in Istanbul, Turkey.

The dinner was great. The table was full of food, and drinks. First, we had soft drinks, then Iraqi pilaf with lamb, rice, and different additions on top. This was followed by sweets, including Iraqi baklava. At the end of the meal, Iraqi tea was served in a little glass, with sugar in the bottom, which you needed to stir before drinking. They also added some special ingredients called "hil," which gave the tea a good taste.

We had a good time, socializing, making jokes, laughing, and watching T.V. Sami asked me if I also spoke Farsi. I said that I didn't, but Col. Z. jokingly suggested that I could learn it with no problem in three months. I replied that it was a good timetable for me, and I would do it. Our Iraqi hosts told us that the singers and performers were Iraqi gypsies, called in Iraq "kawiliya" or "hajars," who travel all over the country. Like most gypsies, they like music and their musicians are famous. That was another bit of Iraqi culture we learned about that evening. We came back to the Unit about 11:30 p.m. in a good mood.

On September 1, the situation in Najaf was relatively calm. As-Sadr visited the shrine of Imam Ali in Najaf for the first time since the cease-fire had been declared between his supporters and the U.S. and Iraqi troops. As-Sadr appealed to his supporters throughout Iraq to stop fighting while the transformation of his movement into the political force was underway.

On September 2, I went to the legal office in the morning. They hadn't received a reply yet on my U.S. citizenship issue. Cpt. P. and his colleagues said that they would try to speak to Immigration Agency representatives. I am supposed to stop by at the end of next week to hear their reply. On the way to my office, I met several Air Force personnel who just arrived in Iraq yesterday. I asked about their first impressions of the country and one said, "It is dirty, dusty, but livable." Another person said, "I like it." They added that, as members of the U.S. Air Force, they were supposed to be in Iraq for only four months. Other service members are usually deployed at least nine to twelve months in the country.

Chapter 15

Escalation of Hostage Taking

Also **on September 2,** news was received that seven hostages from India, Kenya and Egypt were released the previous Wednesday in Iraq. These truck drivers had been kidnapped on July 21 by a group calling itself "The Holders of the Black Banners." The Kuwait and Gulf Link Transport Co. said that it paid $500,000 to secure the release of its employees a day after a video showed the site of the purported killing of twelve Nepalese workers kidnapped in Iraq. The video showed the seven hostages standing against a wall as a masked militant went down the line shaking each captive's hand, giving him a hug, and handing him a Quran and other religious materials. A voice in the background warned "all countries that work with occupiers of the black destiny awaiting them in Iraq if they continue with the work."

Meanwhile, the French hostage crisis persisted with Arab leaders and Muslims worldwide trying to help save journalists Christian Chesnot and Georges Malbrunot, who disappeared August 19 on their way from Baghdad to the southern city of Najaf. The Islamic Army of Iraq, the militant group claimed to be holding the two, demanded that France abolish its ban on Muslim headscarves in public schools. The general attitude of the Arab region toward France is positive, because of the "French government's opposition to the U.S. led war in Iraq and because France is generally pursuing pro-Arab policies," according to some Arab commentators.

On September 3, I am in the office. Several military convoys are waiting to leave, and we are making all the necessary preparations.

On September 4, Sheik Al-Khalafi, who is an aide to radical Shiite cleric Muqtada As-Sadr, denounced the kidnapping of the two French journalists in Iraq and appealed for their release.

Meanwhile, hopes for their release were raised further Friday, when Abdus-Salam Al-Qubeisi, an official with the Association of Muslim Scholars, said the Frenchmen's lives were no longer in danger, and it was only a matter of time before they would be freed. The association is a Sunni clerical organization with alleged ties to insurgents.

While in the southern city of Najaf an official ceasefire between U.S. and Iraqi government forces and supporters of Muqtada As-Sadr is still in place; it is believed that the majority of As-Sadr's militia has returned to Baghdad with their weapons. The situation in the northern Iraqi city of Samarra has become complicated over the last few months. The insurgents in Samarra have assassinated the U.S.-picked leaders and anybody suspected of collaborating with them. Thus, Samarra has become the latest no-go zone for Iraqi National Guard and American troops, and this is the time when preparations have begun for Iraq's nationwide general election scheduled for January.

At the same time, it seems that the U.S. military is avoiding an open military confrontation after the mixed results of fighting in Najaf and Fallujah. That fighting might have attracted more people to the insurgents' side, with U.S. casualties nearing 1,000 killed and many more wounded. Preference is being given at this time to the behind the scenes negotiations between the government of the Interim Prime Minister Al-Allawi and prominent religious moderate leaders and influential organizations such as sheiks or the Muslim Clerics Association of Iraq.

The overall security situation remains uncertain and unpredictable. More and more new trouble spots are emerging, including the northern area of the country in cities like Samarra, Kirkuk and Mosul, which had been considered to be relatively safe areas so far. A few days ago, a powerful car explosion in the Mosul area killed and wounded scores of people.

On September 5, I have a day off. I do a lot of exercising and running.

On September 6, I am back in the office. Several truck drivers, part of a military escort, visit our office. They are asking questions about the date and time of their departure, accident situation, etc. Then I continue to work on written translations that were assigned to me, trying to finish them amid other issues that we had to resolve. I have already completed the translation into Arabic, and now I am finishing the Turkish part of it.

Later, soldiers from another trans unit come over and ask me to help, because they had an accident involving Iraqi and Turkish drivers. I talk to them, and then we manage to calm them down. They were concerned with several issues that needed to be explained.

Meanwhile, I see our local translator Raed, who works for our Civil Affairs Unit. He says that another translator, Firas, was recently kidnapped, beaten and released only after he paid them ten thousand dollars in ransom. So, from now on, Raed, Firas and Sami—our Iraqi translators—are going to stay in the Unit until the security situation improves and it is safe for them to commute between the base and their homes. They characterize the situation as very dangerous.

As an indication of the unstable security situation, reportedly there were 1,100 U.S. forces injured in August. During that month, 66 U.S. service members were killed in Iraq, according to the Defense Department, as reported in the "Stars and Stripes" newspaper of Monday September 6, 2004.

On September 7, I complete the translation on which I was working both in Arabic and Turkish, and I give it to the Unit that had requested it.

On September 8, fighting erupts again in the Baghdad area's Sadr city between U.S. troops and Shiite militiamen loyal to rebel cleric Muqtada As-Sadr. As of Tuesday, 36 persons including one U.S. soldier were killed and 200 civilians were wounded. In the Baghdad area, six U.S. troops were killed in separate incidents. Thus, the total comes to 1,000 U.S. troops killed and 7,000 injured since the beginning of military operations in Iraq, according to official estimates.

Meanwhile, U.S. air strikes target Fallujah again.

On September 9, I have an interesting conversation with Sgt. S. from the Civil Affairs Unit. He is 53 years old, and a veteran of the First Gulf War. His term in Iraq is ending in the beginning of October, and he is going back home to the U.S. He says that he is not planning to come back to Iraq ever again, because he is very tired. In his opinion, "The situation is very uncertain, the right decisions are not being made, and adequate resources are not being provided to fight the insurgency in Iraq." According to S., "It is not clear if we are losing or winning the war on terror, and the one thousand dead U.S. troops is a sad fact." All this is his personal opinion. Now he would like to go home, to work in the yard and around the house, and to spend time with his family. I said in reply that one of the main problems is a lack of basic understanding of the region by the U.S. troops. In order for the U.S. to succeed in the region or in any foreign policy making process we need strong experts with a real and extensive knowledge in that particular area, experts who can give the right advice and recommendations to the administration.

For example, as Sgt. S. mentioned, even for the Civil Affairs Unit, which is usually helping and giving out different kinds of assistance, it was difficult to do its job. This was because of the lack of a friendly environment in the country and adequate resources for successful implementation of the missions. It was clear that it would not be possible to win the hearts and minds of the Iraqi people only through military means. There should be a mixture of military operations, diplomacy, political process, and cultural and educational interaction, etc. This has to be done by the people who really understand the local culture, customs and psychology.

On September 10, I spend all day in the office doing paper work and written translations. Sgt. D. is on duty in the office, scheduling outgoing military convoys.

On September 11, I have to take care of my bank account, which has changed. It is possible that I will be working soon only with the Civil Affairs Unit. Before, I was helping virtually any military unit that might have needed my help, which I found interesting but tiring and unpredictable from the standpoint of security. At the Civil Affairs Unit, I also go off base regularly, but at least I know beforehand when this will happen, and each mission is usually well prepared.

As of September 12, there has been a lot of violence during the weekend, mainly in the Baghdad area and the Green Zone, where the U.S. Embassy and many other foreign embassies are located. A total of 37 persons were killed in several major incidents in the Baghdad area, and 59 were killed across Iraq. In those violent attacks, more than 200 were wounded—more than half of them in the Baghdad area —and the victims were mostly Iraqis. The attacks on U.S. troops are continuing on a regular basis across the country. It seems that the security situation lately has deteriorated even more. Last night, our military convoy was turned back. The reason was that the roads were too dangerous. We have also been under intense mortar and rocket attacks on the base in recent days. One soldier was badly wounded while asleep in a tent on the airfield; he lost two arms and a leg as a mortar round landed and exploded next to him. The military command has ordered soldiers to wear protective armor vest, but they really can protect only in certain situations.

While the cease-fire between supporters of As-Sadr and the U.S. military and Iraqi government forces is still being formally observed in the southern city of Najaf and As-Sadr city of Baghdad, sporadic fighting continues. Likewise, there is continuing violence in the areas of the so-called "Sunni-triangle" and the "triangle of death." In Najaf and As-Sadr city, mediation to achieve a cease-fire was possible mainly because of the substantial influence of Ayatollah Ali As-Sistani, the most respected leader of Iraq's Shiite majority. In another incident, 37 Iraqis, mostly young, were killed when a U.S. helicopter fired on a disabled U.S. Bradley fighting vehicle, as Iraqis swarmed around it, cheering, throwing stones and waving the black and yellow sunburst banner of one of Iraq's terrorist organizations.

The "Tawhid and Jihad," a militant group linked to Al-Qaida

and led by Jordanian-born Abu Musaib Az-Zarqawi carried out the weekend's coordinated campaign of violence in the Baghdad area, according to a statement by that organization. Since the latest intensive violence, the military stores at the base PX and BX are closed; military personnel are ordered to wear protective vests and helmets, and additional security measures are in place at the gates and major points of the base.

Chapter 16

The Constructive Role of Iraq's Top Shiite Leader Ayatollah Ali As-Sistani

Ayatollah Ali As-Sistani is one of the most influential Shiite leaders in Iraq. Other major leaders include Ayatollah Achaq Fiyad Bashir An-Najafi and Muhamed Said Al-Hakim. Ali Sistani's life was difficult during the previous regime. Although his stance is the most liberal—particularly regarding involvement in politics he adheres to the traditional line, "but without the domination of the Islamic Law (Fiqh) and rules. This policy differs from that of the leader of the 1979 Islamic Revolution in Iran, the late Ayatollah Khomeini, mainly in the fact that As-Sistani does not believe in the principle of interference of religion into politics, as did Khomeini and his followers. The "Islamic factor" still plays an important role in the current political and social life of Iran; it is a central element of the Iranian theological government. Ali Sistani's liberal method drew a lot of criticism from the most radical young members of the Shiite community, including Muqtada As-Sadr, the son of Ayatollah Muhamed Sadiq As-Sadr, who was killed by the previous Iraqi regime. Generally, Sistani represents the conservative traditional Shiite viewpoint. It consists mainly of representatives from the Iraqi Shiite leadership who were born in Iran and influenced by the Iranian theological teachings. At the same time, this younger generation of the radical Shiites, demand the authority of Arabs by origin.

Ayatollah Ali As-Sistani was born in 1930 in the Eastern Iranian city of Mashhad, where he received his early education. He continued his education with such distinguished theologians and teachers as Hussein Al-Brujurdi and other Shiite authorities. In 1951, he completed his religious studies under the honorable Imam Al-Hakim,

Ayatollah Ash-Sheikh Hussein Al-Hali, and Al-Imam Al-Khawi. Ali Sistani was actively involved in research and lectured students in the Najaf area. He has written extensively on religious studies.

After the second Gulf War, the regime of Saddam Hussein managed to suppress the Shiite uprising that broke out among Iraqi conservatives. As-Sistani, along with a group of religious theologians, was arrested and put in prison. He was later released.

In 1992, As-Sistani became one of the top Shiite authorities in Iraq. According to a representative of the U.N. in Iraq, Ayatollah Ali As-Sistani did not play a direct role in selecting the cabinet members of the coalition government, but he has been a link in the process that secured the negotiations related to the formation of the temporary government.

On September 13 and 14, I am working with an Iraqi colonel and a major trained by the U.S. Army as a part of a future U.S. exit strategy. Two American officers, Maj. M. and Capt. S., are showing Col. Rahman and Maj. Salem the fuel distribution system. The details of the technological process and the purposes of different kinds of fuel are explained to our Iraqi colleagues, who have also served in the military of the previous Iraqi regime. Special attention is paid to explaining the difference between the fuel distribution systems of the U.S. Army and the previous Iraqi Army. We also visit the office where all the paperwork is being prepared for those U.S. soldiers, coalition forces members, and Iraqi National Guardsmen killed in Iraq. Then, we visit the place where the soldiers' bodies are kept before they are sent to their final resting spots. The bodies of the U.S. military personnel are sent back to the States, while Iraqis are handed over to family members, if they are available.

On September 16, We are visited by several Iraqi Kurds who seek help in recovering their abandoned truck near Tikrit city. They were part of a U.S. military convoy that was coming from the mainly Kurdish controlled area of Zakhu. This was supposed to be the final destination to unload their cargo.

A car bomb exploded Tuesday on a busy street near the Baghdad police headquarters. Iraqis were waiting there to apply for jobs, when gunmen opened fire on a van carrying police home from work in Baqouba; at least 59 people were killed and 114 others were wounded.

Also on Tuesday, during clashes between U.S. troops and insurgents, at least eight civilians were killed and eighteen were wounded in the western city of Ramadi. Ramadi is a predominantly Sunni city, where the residents harbor a high degree of anti-American sentiment. U.S. troops are frequently under attack in Ramadi. That same day, according to the military, three American soldiers were killed and eight others were wounded across Iraq during a 24-hour period. The casualties were particularly in the Baghdad area, but also in the northern city of Mosul and other locations.

As of Monday, the Defense Department estimates that 1,012 members of the U.S. military have died in Iraq since the beginning of military operations in March 2003 and 7,245 have been wounded. Also, from April 2003 to May 2004, 710 Iraqi policemen were killed out of a total force of 130,000. This is a result of the campaign conducted by gunmen and insurgents across Iraq against those that they call "collaborators" and "traitors."

While I am writing these memoirs, there is a mortar attack in the housing area close to our office. Fortunately, no casualties occur at this time. The territory surrounding the office, which is located at the military convoy staging area, has frequently been targeted by the insurgents.

Meanwhile, U.S. Secretary of State Colin Powell—in response to a question from Senator Susan Collins, a Republican from Maine–said, "It turned out that we have not found any stockpiles. Moreover, I think it is unlikely that we will find any stockpiles."

Also **on September 16**, at around 3 p.m. an alarm goes off. I am checking my e-mail but everybody has to go into the shelter until the all—clear sounds. By 5:52 p.m., the all clear signal still has not sounded. Everybody remains inside the shelter. This has been one of the longest alarms we have had. Something truly serious may have happened. We don't always know about every incident that takes place in our immediate area. Finally, at 5:54, the all—clear is signaled.

On September 17, I am in the office at the military convoy staging area. According to news reports and first—hand accounts from soldiers returning from their missions with the convoys things are not going as well as expected. The U.S. Department of Defense says that since the beginning of military operations in Iraq 1,018 U.S. service members died in the country. This figure includes three civilian employees.

The main problem in Iraq remains insurgency—local as well as international fighters. Many experts and military commanders are starting to realize that it is time to get rid of illusions about the security situation in the country and pay serious attention to this reality.

Today, we learn that yesterday's alarm was the result of a possible rocket or mortar attack, which was contained. It took almost three hours to eliminate the source of the attack, which shows its sophistication. To eliminate such attacks, our military normally uses combat helicopters, which can identify and destroy the insurgents and their logistical bases in many, but not all, situations.

On September 18, I meet C., 55-year-old U.S. Army officer who is currently working with an Engineering Unit. C. served in Vietnam and is now completing his mission in Iraq. He is preparing to resign next June and spend more time with his grandchildren.

C. says that the situation with the insurgency is not clear. He thinks that many Arab and Muslim countries, including Saudi Arabia, are opposed bringing democracy and the emancipation of women to Iraq. According to C., who is a native Texan, it is not safe at all outside of the U.S. military bases. In fact, the security situation has worsened lately. He says that the Americans can't stay in Iraq forever. Iraqis have to take things in their own hands. Indirectly, he reflected an uncertainty about winning the war in Iraq.

Chapter 17

The Uncertainty of Winning the War in Iraq, and Its Global Implications

Later, when I returned to the States after my year-long Iraqi experience I got the opportunity to talk to American government representatives and U.S. citizens about the war. I realized that the American public had many doubts and misperceptions about the war in Iraq from the very beginning. Those sentiments were growing as U.S. casualties mounted. The end of the war was not visible any time soon, and there was no clear exit strategy. It was also clear that the war had damaged the relationships of the U.S. with its traditional allies in Europe and elsewhere, including its NATO partners.

Also, many people, both internationally and in the United States, did not accept the justification for the war in Iraq, given the fact that no weapons of mass destruction were found and no clear connection was established between the former regime of Saddam Hussein and Al-Qaida, which were the two main reasons for the war.

Why not North Korea, for example. North Korea would seem like a more logical country to punish, because it already had weapons of mass destruction and was openly challenging the international community? Moreover, some people held the opinion that a change in the geopolitical map of the Middle East would do more harm than good to U.S. interests for several reasons. Saddam Hussein was a dictator, but in reality his secular government was some kind of counterbalance to governments such as the Iranian Shiite clerical regime. The Iranian regime posed a much more obvious challenge to U.S. interests in the region through their network of morally and financially supported groups such as Hezbollah (in Arabic, the Party of God). According to various estimates, Hezbollah, which is on the U.S. terrorist list, has about 100,000 well trained and well-armed militants with high morale that are ready to die for their cause. Their main ideology is militant Islam with a great deal of hostility to the U.S., Israel and the West. The Islamic jihad and the definition of the "Islamic Umma" have a very practical meaning for Hezbollah members. The organization is based in the southern part of Lebanon.

Secondly, the religious Shiite clerics who returned to Iraq from exile, mainly from neighboring Iran, had close relationships with the current Iranian theocratic authorities. Thus, it remains to be seen to what extent the Iraqi Shiite leaders are sincere in their cooperation with the U.S. and coalition forces. Finally, some are of the opinion that the war has turned Iraq into a real training camp for terrorists who can threaten any country of the world, including the U.S.

Considering the fact that Syria and Iran are virtually surrounded by U.S. and coalition forces in Iraq, Afghanistan, Kuwait and some former Soviet Central Asian republics, is it realistic to expect that they would not be trying to destabilize the situation in Iraq? The logic is simple; the longer the U.S. and coalition troops are bogged down in Iraq the lower the chances are that military action might be taken against these countries that are hostile to the U.S.'s interests.

It is also possible that Syria and even Iran are financing the other local Iraqi and international insurgents, including the Al-Qaida network fighters over and above those that are already known, such as the Shiite "Mehdi Army" of Muqtada As-Sadr, which is financed and supported by Iran.

There were claims by the British that Iran was involved in the recent killings of British soldiers in the southern Iraqi city of Basra through its Hezbollah militants. Other Arab and Muslim countries are apparently supporting the Iraqi insurgency, mainly on the grassroots level. At the same time, some major powers, such as Russia - a member of the U.N. Security Council- are reluctant to support possible sanctions against both Iran and Syria.

At the same time, events in the West and East show that the Islamic organizations became more active and more aggressive. Thus, the global implications of the war in Iraq do not look positive so far.

Chapter 18

No Clear Strategy

On September 19, I talk to our local Iraqi translator, Firas, who is assigned to the Civil Affairs Unit. He says, "the security situation is getting worse because the U.S. is not thinking ahead." What he most likely means is that there is not a clear advance plan for the U.S.'s policy in Iraq. Therefore, the number of "bad guys" is increasing, and the "bad guys" are finding it increasingly easy to fight the Americans. As Firas indicates, the reason is that many U.S. soldiers are inexperienced in combat situations; so many necessary actions are falling by the wayside in Iraq. For example, he says that U.S. troops were supposed to seal off the borders of Iraq and not let the foreign fighters come in; this did not happen.

I ask, "Was it even possible to seal the borders, given their extensive length and the country's proximity to neighboring countries?" Firas answers, "Yes, it is possible, because Saddam Hussein closed the borders during his time." He goes on to explain a method that groups like Al-Qaida use to recruit fighters. He says, "If I was a "bad guy," I would try to convince my friend to join the fight against U.S. troops. I would reason that it is easy and a kill could earn us $5,000. Initially, my friend might reject the idea, saying that he couldn't do it because he could get killed. In that case, I would suggest it to him over and over. Finally, I would show him the money I earned. At last, my friend would be convinced. He would either join one of the insurgent groups fighting for ideological reasons, or he would become a member of one of the many criminal groups that make money by attacking American and Iraqi government troops or kidnapping for ransom."

According to Firas, the myth that the U.S. army was unbeatable was gradually being dismissed, because the fact was that there were as many U.S. soldiers getting killed as there were local and foreign fighters emerging and joining the anti-American cause. He also mentioned that the need for money makes many people join the ranks of the insurgency. Organizations such as Al-Qaida are willing to pay for their cause.

I ask, "Where are these organizations getting their financial resources?" Firas says, "There are a lot of charities and organizations--even some individual countries--that do not want to see the U.S. succeed in Iraq. Right now, nobody likes the United States."

As I mentioned before, Firas has just been released from captivity. A group had kidnapped and tortured him. He was only released after he paid a $10,000 ransom. He thought that they were going to kill him. At that time, his only hope was God. He constantly prayed, promising God that he would be a better Muslim. According to Firas, he had not been a good Muslim before this incident; he had never prayed or gone to the Mosque. After a while, his captors suddenly suggested that they would release him if he paid a ransom. Firas believes that God heard his prayers and helped him in his time of difficulty.

I agreed with him, but I also indicated the possibility that the group had commercial motivations. In other words, it was trying to get money by kidnapping people. Organizations such as Al-Qaida and Jordanian born Abu Musaib Az-Zarqawi's Tawhid and Jihad group were fighting mainly for political and ideological purposes, such as the withdrawal of American and coalition forces from Iraq. If their demands were not met, they usually killed hostages: U.S. and coalition troops, local Iraqis, and foreign and local contractors working for the U.S. and coalition troops. Presently, more than 100 foreigners are being held by various insurgent groups in Iraq. With time, this number will probably increase.

The most recent abductions include three contractors--two Americans and one Briton--who were kidnapped from their homes in Baghdad. They were working for "Gulf Services," a Middle Eastern company. The captors are demanding the release of female inmates detained in the infamous U.S-controlled Abu Ghraib prison of Baghdad and the British run Umm Qasr prison. Abu Ghraib is known for the scandal related to the sexual abuse of the male prisoners, which got widespread international publicity and caused significant damage to the prestige of the U.S. Army. Later, the concerns about the treatment of the prisoners there would double. The following soldiers were eventually charged in a military court due to their abuse of many prisoners in the jail: Specialist Charles Graner, Staff Sgt. Ivan Frederic, Pfc. Lyndie England, and Specialist Sabrina Harman. At the forefront of the investigation and trials were photographs that surfaced that revealed how the soldiers kept Iraqi prisoners on leashes, in abusive sexual positions. Newspapers described the soldiers as "having a good time."

That same evening, I talk to Lt. Col. I. of the Civil Affairs Unit. He says that the current security situation is not clear. The U.S. bombings in Fallujah are not accurate and are creating more enemies than friends. Firas had mentioned that those bombings usually killed innocent civilians—women, children, and elderly citizens.

On September 20, I am in the office at the military convoy staging area. I talk to Salman, a local Iraqi translator, about some cultural issues. He says that it is very difficult for a foreigner to get married in Iraq. For example, he mentioned how a local Iraqi family had refused to allow their daughter to marry an Egyptian man, even though he had lived in an Iraqi village for the past 14 years. According to Salman, it is even hard for an Iraqi woman to simply marry outside of her tribe.

Chapter 19

Financial Motives for Working in Iraq

The absence of a clear exit strategy and the demand for workers led the authorities to hire many contractors who lacked both experience and positive moral incentives. These contractors were, in some cases, completely ignorant of the local culture. This ignorance, along with the psychological and cultural peculiarities of the international contractors, resulted in numerous incidents.

On September 22, there is an incident in the KBR (subsidiary of Halliburton company) contractor yard. At about 1:00 or 2:00 a.m., a KBR representative gets mad at a Turkish truck driver and smashes his truck's side window with a metal object. We think we know who did it. There have been at least three similar incidents so far, involving the same person. The commander of our unit, Major B., talks to one of the KBR supervisors, and he is promised that their management will take the appropriate actions. The help that many foreign contractors are giving us is tremendous, and some are getting killed and wounded along with U.S. soldiers and contractors.

Today we receive information that one of the American contractors, Eugene Armstrong, 62, was decapitated by the Tawhid and Jihad organization. He had been kidnapped from his home in Baghdad. Armstrong was working for the Gulf Services Company, which is based in the Middle East. His captors were demanding the release of all female inmates kept in Abu Ghraib and Umm Qasr prisons.

I am asked to look at pictures of three truck drivers who had recently been decapitated. Because I deal with many contractors through my work, and I am asked whether I can identify their bodies. One of them had a tattoo and, although it was very unclear, I still could identify Arabic script. That is why I suggest that they were not

Turkish contractors, as it was thought, but Kurdish Sunni Muslims from the Kurdish Democratic Party, who had recently been abducted. Another possibility is that they were members of the Iraqi National guard who were also abducted recently. It is difficult to identify their faces because decapitation causes an outflow of blood that causes faces to change significantly.

At about 11:30 a.m., there is a mortar attack close to our area. We also receive information that a second American, Jack Hensley, was executed by the same Tawhid and Jihad organization. Hensley had been abducted earlier by that group. The slaughter of the second American hostage had been confirmed by the Islamic website. As of Monday, according to the Defense Department, 1,032 members of the U.S. military have died since the beginning of the Iraq war in March 2003.

On September 23, I call my employer's representative in the Balad area of Iraq. I need to complete some personal issues back in the United States.

Chapter 20

Security Situation Remains a Challenge

The U.S. and Iraqi government forces continue to face a fierce resistance from the insurgency in Iraq. Reportedly, it prompted the Pentagon to begin spending money from a $25 billion emergency fund that administration officials earlier said would not be needed this year. A large portion of money that was set aside for reconstruction is now being redirected because of the unstable security situation.

The war in Iraq is costing about $4.4 billion a month, and that amount is expected to increase. According to Pentagon officials, as of June, the total cost of the war in Iraq reached $86.2 billion. Meanwhile, the same sources report that, as of September 21, 1,037 members of the U.S. military have died since the beginning of the Iraq war in March 2003.

As of September 24, the political future of the country still remains uncertain. This is reflected by the latest concern expressed by influential Shiite leader Ayatollah Ali As-Sistani. He says that the future Iraqi government might not be represented by a sufficient number of Shiite Iraqis. There is still a long way to go to achieve stability in a country that has historically been represented by three main groups: Shiites, Sunnis, and Kurds.

On September 25, I am in the office at the military convoy staging area. We have had several visitors this morning. Two Egyptians came in, one of them needing to call Kuwait because he had some kind of court problem there. A Turkish truck driver asked for his brother's report on a lost truck carrying JP8-type fuel for aircrafts, near the city of Samarra. The truck was left there after an accident, and his brother had just been released from the hospital. A KBR company representative is going to take them to the hospital to try to get an incident report.

On September 26, there is a rocket attack next to the Civil Affairs Unit building where we are staying.

On September 27, there is a mortar attack at the military convoy staging area. The all-clear siren sounds only 30 minutes later. We are told that there were casualties at the contractors' yard.

On September 28, I am trying to organize a soccer team among the soldiers and contractors.

I love playing soccer, and I thought it would be a good way to relax physically and psychologically from the tough realities of the war. We play in the evening. At this point, we have two local Iraqi translators, two Turkish workers-contractors, and me. Later, our team will grow and include some of our soldiers and other contractors. An article about our unusual initiative in the war zone was published in the military newspaper. It presented me as an organizer of the soccer team on the base. When I wrote my wife to tell her that we organized a soccer team, she became concerned that I could get killed while playing.

On September 29, we receive information that two Egyptian engineers were kidnapped from their offices. They were working for a company called Iraqina, which is affiliated with the Egyptian company Orascom. The engineers were involved in providing telephone and other communications services in Iraq, and their abduction occurred in Baghdad. During the last three weeks, the city has seen an unusual wave of kidnappings that use the same method. Previously, the majority of the kidnappings took place in certain dangerous areas. Lately, however, kidnappers have been active specifically in the Baghdad area. Two Americans and one British contractor were abducted separately from their Baghdad homes. The Americans were subsequently executed, while the fate of British hostage Kenneth Begley is still uncertain. The motives behind the kidnappings of the two Egyptian engineers are not known. They were taken in a black car in an unknown direction.

At the same time, unconfirmed information indicates the kidnapping of four more Egyptian contractors. They were working for a construction company in the Qaim region in the West of Iraq. The Egyptians were kidnapped with the same method as used with the previous two. All of them were abducted from their work place.

I also had an interesting conversation with Sergeant A. today. I found out that he is a Native American from the Apache tribe. This tribe is scattered across several states, such as California, Nevada, Idaho, Oklahoma, and New Mexico. The majority, including A's relatives, live on reservations. They are trying to preserve their traditions and their style of life.

A. says that the Apache tribe is one of the largest Native American tribes in the United States. According to him, there are Mountain Apaches, Desert Apaches, and Plain Apaches. A. belongs to the Desert Apaches, which are traditionally good warriors. This is why A. says that he is bored—the people of his tribe are not afraid of death and are always looking for a fight, but here, he cannot go outside of the base. According to their teachings, death takes them to a new level of the "circle." He says that the Apache tribe believes in the Sun, Moon, and Stars as their God. At the same time, he is a practicing Christian and attends church regularly. He is trying to balance Christianity and his traditional culture. The Apaches begin their warrior training when they are only eight years-old, and they are always looking for a "good and meaningful death;" They cannot wait until "death comes to them." Also, the Apaches are typically good hunters. For all those reasons, A. says that he would prefer to be outside of the base doing a dangerous job.

The Apache teaching holds that God is the Sun and the Moon. Every person should go through a certain circle to his or her Star. Stars represent their ancestors. After death, Apaches join their Stars on the so-called "fire camp on the Star." Each person has his or her own Star.

A. says that most of the U.S. soldiers would prefer to stay on the base, rather than go outside. The main reason is that most of them have families back home, and they do not want to risk their lives.

Sergeant S., who is from the same unit, prefers to stay on the base. In his opinion, Islam is growing worldwide—including in the United States—because it is a religion which says that if you do certain things, you will go to heaven. Sergeant S. is a Christian and believes that the violence in Iraq will continue until Jesus Christ comes back on earth; only then will peace prevail. Until then, according to him, even if the United States sends a million troops to Iraq, the security situation will not change for the better. He says that those who do not believe in God will go to hell.

In the evening, I talk to one of our local translators, Raid. He has just returned from his home in Balad. His friend has a business making pictures on Haifa Street in the center of Baghdad. This street has witnessed plenty of violence lately and is currently closed to traffic and pedestrians.

Raid recounts a recent incident in which he saw Iraqi insurgents shooting from the roof of a nearby building. They were targeting an American tank on Haifa Street. The American soldiers sporadically shot back. Raid says that he was lucky to be able to get away in his car.

Raid indicates that the security situation is worsening every day. The people are angry about everyday violence and killings. He says that the number of local and foreign fighters is increasing. He is worried that the situation will become volatile.

It seems that many military operations are being conducted by the coalition forces, as new fighters are filling the ranks of the insurgents. The increasing violence also encourages ordinary Iraqis to turn more and more to their traditional values and religion. The "Islamic factor" is becoming a buffer and form of protection against the presence of foreign troops, external and local fighters, and basic criminal groups. At the same time, religion is being used by the different militant organizations as the ideological basis for their activities against the coalition forces and the newly-emerging Iraqi government.

If the volatile security situation persists, it is likely that more and more Iraqis who feel unprotected and economically disadvantaged will become vulnerable for recruitment into the ranks of the political insurgency or criminal groups. If this happens, it would be a major setback for U.S. interests in the region and particularly for the establishment of democracy in Iraq. The current state of affairs in Iraq is very unsatisfactory.

Also, there is Shiite resistance in Sadr City, Najaf, and Karbala. In addition, there are signs of insurgency in the "Sunni triangle," in the Anbar province, which includes such cities as Ramadi, Samarra, and Fallujah. This situation is being complicated by the so-called "Kurdish factor" in the North of the country. Recently, the leaders of the main Kurdish political parties announced that Arabs needed to leave certain areas, particularly around Kirkuk, in order to populate it with ethnic Kurds. All these factors make the security situation extremely unpredictable, and they could lead to the possibility of civil war, chaos, and an uncontrollable insurgency.

On September 30, a Pakistani truck driver comes in and asks for an incident report. He was part of a U.S. military convoy coming from the North through the Taji area. They were attacked near a bridge by the insurgents. He lost his truck, and his partner was wounded and taken to a hospital.

I have dinner with Lieutenant Colonels I. and P. They say that the elections scheduled for Iraq in January cannot be considered seriously, given the current unstable conditions in the country. They also say that, according to the U.S. administration, "it is going to be partial elections, meaning that they would not cover certain geographic areas." Those areas are actually "no-go zones" for the U.S. and coalition forces and are controlled by insurgents.

According to I. and P., it looks like the insurgency was not expected after the fall of Saddam Hussein's regime. What can be done in these circumstances? Send more troops? P. replies that the best solution would be to have an Iraq leader to whom Iraqis would listen. Otherwise, current Prime Minister Ayad Allawi, or others who would be similarly supported by the United States, would be seen by the Iraqis as mere puppets of the foreign governments. Their main point was that Iraqis were not yet ready for the elections and for democracy in general.

As far as the insurgency is concerned, many military commanders, including General John Abizaid (the top commander in Iraq), acknowledge that foreign fighters make up a small percentage of the insurgency. According to military sources, the Iraqi insurgency is mainly local and consists predominantly of supporters of Saddam Hussein's former regime and Baath Party members. Immediately after the fall of Hussein, they left, mainly for Syria. Later, they returned to Iraq, bringing their money and experience to the insurgency. Many of them are from the top military leadership of the former regime and have extensive military experience, including years of participation in the Iran-Iraq war. They are trying to do everything they can to disrupt the upcoming elections and the efforts of the U.S. and coalition forces.

In the evening, a concert is held on our base. I go there with Lt. Col. I. It is a nice concert, and it helps my morale to get away from the realities of war.

On October 1, it is reported that 35 Iraqi children were among the civilians who were killed on Thursday by a series of bombs that struck while U.S. troops were handing out candy at the inauguration of a new sewage treatment plant in a Baghdad neighborhood. Earlier, a suicide blast killed a U.S. soldier and two Iraqis.

At least four people were killed and 16 were injured by a car bomb in the northern city of Tal Afar. Also on Thursday, Al-Jazeera showed a video of 10 new hostages seized in Iraq by militants.

According to Lt. Gen. Ricardo Sanchez, a top U.S. commander in the region, troops are getting "mixed messages" from Iraqis; Iraqis say they need coalition forces in Iraq, but at the same time, they do not want them to be there.

The reason for the mixed feelings is probably because there are strong anti-American and anti-coalition sentiments in the society.

Nevertheless, the Iraqis realize that there is a real danger of civil war and chaos if the coalition forces leave in the near future. They are concerned that, as a result of the security vacuum, they might not be able to handle the situation themselves.

October 2. On my way to work, I talk to a 33-year veteran of U.S. military, Pilot N., who is in his mid-fifties. He says that he is going to retire because of what was going on in Iraq. According to him, the security situation is getting worse day by day. I ask his opinion about where this is leading. In reply, he asks, "What do you think?" I say that it is not clear to me yet. N. says that Iraq has a variety of ethnicities and religions, which make it very complex. He cites, for example, how Kurds admire current U.S. President Bush and are generally positive about the United States. N. says that they would not even mind becoming the 51st U.S. state, if that was possible.

Chapter 21

Upcoming U.S. Presidential Elections and Their Possible Impact on the Situation in Iraq

We are closely following the debates between the main candidates for the U.S. presidential elections. Currently, they are President George W. Bush and Senator John Kerry. Many of the military personnel and contractors that I talk to believe that, depending on who is going to become the new president, the policy in the Middle East, particularly in terms of troop deployment in Iraq, might change.

I watched part of yesterday's first TV debate between President Bush and Senator Kerry. The Senator made his points more clear than he has in the past. He talked about issues, such as the situation in Iraq, the connection between Saddam Hussein and Al-Qaida, weapons of mass destruction (WMD) in Iraq, an exit strategy, the plan "to win the peace after the initial military operation in Iraq," the absence of careful planning, etc. As the polls subsequently showed, Senator Kerry did better than Bush. Some 43% of viewers were in favor of Kerry and 28% in favor of Bush. The remainders were undecided.

Meanwhile, according to government figures, there have been at least 134 officially reported deaths and 858 reports of injuries involving workers from the United States and other countries since the invasion in March 2003.

At the same time, about 1,052 U.S. military personnel have been killed and more than 7,000 wounded. As the casualties are mounting, the popularity of the war among both U.S. soldiers and ordinary Americans is falling further.

In the evening of **October 3,** we experienced five mortar attacks in less than two hours.

As of October 4, according to the U.S. military, U.S. and Iraqi government troops control about 70% of Samarra. During recent military operations, more than 100 insurgents were killed and 80 were captured. Samarra, along with the cities Fallujah and Ramadi, was a "no go zone." The area was practically controlled by insurgents. Presently, the U.S. and Iraqi forces are trying to reestablish control over these areas before the January elections in Iraq. In Samarra, diplomacy and negotiations with local religious and tribal leaders, and military forces was used. According to U.S. officials, the same tactics will be used in other areas partially or completely controlled by insurgents, including Fallujah, Ramadi, Najaf and As-Sadr City.

On October 5, there is a mortar attack on the military convoy staging area. Several KBR contractors are wounded, including one American female. We go to the area where the mortar landed. It hit a spot between the trailers where the contractors live. The trailers are covered with holes from shrapnel.

On October 6, there is another mortar attack at about 7:00 a.m. Later in the day, I meet a soldier in the bathroom. He is talking to another soldier, and he says that his shoulder was badly injured. He can hardly move his arm, but he says that he wants to go back there again. At 2:20 p.m., two mortars land close to our workplace. It shakes our trailer office.

Chapter 22

U.S. Commanders on the Iraqi Insurgency

According to U.S. military commanders, the insurgency in Iraq consists of four main groups. First, there are the members of Saddam Hussein's former group, who are mainly Iraqi nationalists fighting trying to rebuild secular power lost as a result of the 2003 invasion. The second group consists of Abu Musaib Az-Zarqawi's followers and its allies, including: Tawhid and Jihad, Ansar Al-Islam, the militia of Kurdish Islamic radicals, and Ansar As-Sunna. These groups are predominantly following conservative Islam as practiced in Saudi Arabia. They are mainly anti-Western and fight for the creation of an Islamic state, such as Afghanistan's Taliban regime. Third, there are those who support the creation of a government that is based on Islamic Law (Fikh), such as the government of neighboring Iran. Lastly, there is the Mehdi Army, led by radical Shiite leader Muqtada As-Sadr. He has potentially the largest social and religious base among Iraq's approximately 70% Shiite population. It is mainly concentrated in the southern Shiite holy cities of Najaf, Karbala, Kut, and Sadr City.

Although this is the current perception of the Iraqi insurgency among the top U.S. Commanders, it changes from time to time, depending on the security situation. In my view, the insurgency is also becoming increasingly sophisticated.

In the evening, I am asked to go to the military hospital to help communicate with a Turkish contractor who was wounded when an IED exploded and injured his right arm and side while he was on his way to "Anaconda" air base.

The tent-hospital's room is full of wounded people. I see only one U.S. soldier; the others are mainly Iraqis and Turkish contractors. Some of them are slightly wounded, others more severely. The nurse explains that some of them are Iraqi National Guardsmen. Interestingly, many insurgents are receiving medical treatment in the same room. According to the nurse, after treatment they are going to be interrogated and subsequently jailed.

When I enter, I notice an insurgent who is sleeping. Both of his legs are bandaged above the knees. The nurse explains that he lost his legs when the explosive that he was setting up on the road to fight U.S. troops exploded prematurely, ironically wounding him instead. I stand with my back toward him while interpreting for a contractor. I eventually turn around and notice that the insurgent is looking at me with wide open eyes. He has a strange look. The nurse tells me that he has been quiet and never talks to anyone.

I came to the hospital with Sergeant R. and our local translator, Firaz Abbas. There is a mortar attack while we are in the hospital, and we have to go to a nearby bunker to take cover. It takes a while until the all-clear siren is sounded and we can leave the bunker.

On October 7, we have a Kurdish visitor in the military convoy staging area office. He was part of a U.S. military convoy coming to the "Anaconda" air base when his truck broke down. He is waiting for another military convoy to go to Turkey, where his company is located.

Chapter 23

No Weapons of Mass Destruction

The top U.S. arms inspector, Charles Duelfer, head of the Iraq Survey Group, reported Wednesday that he found no evidence that Iraq produced any weapons of mass destruction after 1991. It was a clear contradiction to the main argument for beginning the war in 2003. At the same time, the point was made that Saddam Hussein might have had the ambition to produce weapons of mass destruction, but did not have a real capability to do so after 1991 as a result of the first Gulf War and devastating UN sanctions.

On October 8, I am asked again to come to the hospital to help with interpreting. I see more wounded U.S. soldiers, including one female. Local wounded Iraqis are placed in different rooms. The doctors say that lately, wounded persons are being kept longer in order to treat them better and to make sure that their wounds are not getting infections. At lunch time there is a mortar attack while I am in the hospital.

On October 10, there is a rocket attack at about 6:00 p.m. About two hours pass until the all clear siren is heard.

On October 11, I talk to two truck drivers, who were part of the military convoys. They say that the security situation on the roads is much worse than it was several months ago. Both of them are Kurds from the northern city of Irbil. They say that in Irbil and Suleymaniya the situation is quiet and stable. These areas are practically controlled by the Kurdish militia, the "Peshmarga", after the first Gulf War. They say that insurgents are targeting anybody on the roads who is cooperating with Americans, especially Kurds.

Chapter 24

Combining Diplomacy with Military Operations

On October 12, it is reported that Muqtada As-Sadr's followers have started to hand in their weapons. This is part of the U.S.-Iraqi strategy of combining military operations with diplomacy, and it follows weeks of fighting between the U.S.-Iraqi forces and As-Sadr's Shiite militia. The fighters are supposed to be compensated for the weapons they are giving up. According to Iraqi police sources, the rates range from $5 for a hand grenade to $1,000 for a heavy-caliber machine gun.

These efforts are being undertaken to make sure that as much territory of Iraq as possible is under U.S.-Iraqi control by the January elections, in order to make them legitimate. For that reason, a new policy of negotiations, coupled with the use of American firepower when necessary, is being pursued. According to U.S. administration officials, most major assaults on insurgent-held Iraq, cities such as Fallujah and Ramadi, will be delayed until after U.S. elections in November.

This information probably indicates that the administration is unwilling to conduct major military operations in Iraq at the height of the U.S. presidential elections; they would lead to increased American casualties which, in turn, might affect the results of the elections.

But the first step towards regaining control of As-Sadr city, one of As-Sadr's strongholds, is definitely a positive sign. If it materializes, the U.S.-led coalition and the Iraqi security forces could concentrate on the most potentially volatile Sunni areas.

At present, the situation seems to be deteriorating. More hostages are being taken, and bombings are occurring on a daily basis.

According to reports, the most recent abductions include one Kurdish translator and a Turkish contractor who worked for the Titan National Security Solutions Company. Reportedly, they were kidnapped in Ramadi, which is about 70 miles west of the capital Baghdad, by the insurgent group Ansar As-Sunna Army. The abductors are demanding that Turkish contractors and companies leave Iraq within three days, as well as the release of all Iraqi prisoners.

In the meantime, the frequent air strikes on insurgent controlled cities, such as Fallujah, seem to be leading to the deaths of both militants and civilians, including women, children, and the elderly. If this is the case, it will most likely fuel anti-American sentiments even further, and they are already high in those areas.

On October 13, U.S. and Iraqi government forces start a new offensive wave against Sunni strongholds in Ramadi and Fallujah. They are raiding mosques in the hopes of finding weapons caches belonging to the insurgents. It is a new element of U.S. military operations. Previously, they avoided entering religious sites, so as not to ignite anti-American sentiments. This time, the U.S. spokesman said they "respect the cultural and religious significance represented by the mosques," but "when insurgents violate the sanctity of the mosque by using the structure for military purposes, the site loses its protective status."

Chapter 25

U.S. Elections and Ongoing Violence in Iraq

On October 14, there is a mortar attack in the morning. We continue to watch the third and last TV debate between Senator John Kerry and President George W. Bush. According to the polls, Democrat Kerry won again over the president. Issues discussed were mainly on domestic policies: the economy, health care, taxes, etc. Many people on the base are carefully following the U.S. presidential campaigns. There is already a feeling that John Kerry is going to win, and there are many questions about how it is going to affect U.S. policy in Iraq.

On October 15, there are military reports of a suicide attack and roadside bombs that killed six U.S. soldiers. Two American soldiers are killed and five are wounded when a suicide driver enters a U.S. military convoy and blows up his car in the northern city of Mosul. Three U.S. deaths occurred late Tuesday, when a roadside bomb exploded near a U.S. military convoy in eastern Baghdad. Another American soldier died in a bombing Wednesday in western Baghdad.

As of Tuesday, the number of U.S. personnel killed reached 1,072, according to the Defense Department. That included three civilians employed by the military.

Meanwhile, tension is reportedly growing between local insurgents and foreign fighters in some areas of the country, particularly in the western city of Fallujah. The city became the target of frequent U.S. air raids against suspected gatherings of followers of the Jordanian born Abu Musaib Az-Zarqawi. His group, Tawhid and Jihad committed a number of beheadings, deadly bombings and attacks across Iraq.

There is a growing indication that local insurgents want the foreigners to leave because they feel that the foreign fighters are distorting the Iraqi resistance. One of those locals is Abu Abdullah Dulaimy, who is the leader of an Iraqi insurgent group called the First Army of Muhammed.

One of the prominent foreign fighters killed recently by local tribesmen was Abdullah Suri, a Syrian and a member of Az-Zarqawi's group. An Iraqi security guard witnessed the killing.

Stepping up air raids in the area will likely attract more people to join the ranks of the insurgents in the coming weeks, because of the inevitability of civilian casualties during air raids. In particular, recent U.S. and Iraqi government raids of mosques and other religious sites in Ramadi, Samarra and other places will likely increase anti-American sentiments and further fuel the insurgency.

The government of Prime Minister Ayad Al-Allawi is increasingly viewed by the majority of Iraqis as a U.S. puppet regime, which is one of the main reasons for the violence and instability. Many think that, until Al-Allawi is removed and Iraqis feel that they are in control of their own government, the violence will likely continue in the foreseeable future with differences in intensity at various stages.

Additionally, some countries, such as Iran and Syria, may be interested in the continuation of violence in Iraq, because as long as the U.S. and coalition forces are stuck in Iraq, they will not be able to move on to Iran or Syria. There are numerous reports indicating that fighters from Iran, Syria and other countries are present in Iraq.

It was reported on Thursday that insurgents managed to penetrate Baghdad's heavily fortified Green Zone and detonated explosives at a market and a popular café, killing four American civilians and six Iraqis. The Green Zone contains the U.S. and Iraqi government headquarters and the embassies of other countries. It was the first bombing inside the compound.

Also **on October 15,** there were two mortar attacks in our area at about 5:30 p.m. and 6:00 p.m.

On October 16, I go to the dining facility for the military convoys and the foreign contractors who are helping them. For the first time, I see a sign on the wall in Arabic, prohibiting Muslims from entering the facility. It is strange, especially because the majority of the foreign contractors are from Turkey and Arab countries, and they are mainly Muslims. This is the only dining facility that has been arranged for them and for the U.S. personnel of the military convoys. A Filipino guard at the entrance tells me that this is a new KBR policy. I am surprised to hear something like that stated for the first time.

I ask the facility manager, who is an American, about the policy. He connects it with the Muslim holiday Ramadan, but the reason is still not clear. If it is about fasting, which Muslims are supposed to observe during the month of Ramadan, naturally that is their personal issue. That could not be a reason to forbid them from entering the facility. I think it is really for security purposes. During Ramadan, the insurgents usually become more active, but this measure is a mistake and obviously unproductive. Why would the KBR company interfere in this kind of issue?

I tell Major B. about the situation. He is the commander of the relevant military unit and is responsible for staging military convoys. B. is upset by the possibility that the Muslim convoy members might be turned away from the dining facility. He says he is going to find out about the situation. In fact, while I am at the facility, I see at least one person who is turned away and not allowed to enter.

On October 17, there are two mortar attacks. Clashes continue between insurgents and U.S. troops in Fallujah. Meanwhile, two U.S. soldiers were killed Saturday, when two Army helicopters crashed in Baghdad. As of Friday, 1,086 members of the U.S. military have died since the beginning of military operations in Iraq in March 2003, according to the Defense Department.

On base Logistics Support Area (LSA) "Anaconda" we continue to experience mortar and rocket attacks daily. Sources say that at least a half dozen soldiers and contractors have been killed and nearly 100 wounded just on this base as the result of mortar attacks since April.

About a month ago, an airman lost both legs and his right arm when a mortar shell was fired onto the base. I think in most cases rockets or mortars land without hitting any particular targets, but sometimes they cause casualties.

Usually after the first round of an attack, the alarm makes a rising sound, signifying the status "red." It means that everybody should take cover inside of the bunkers or hardened buildings. When the loudspeakers carry the announcement "yellow," it means that a "necessary movement for appropriate personnel is allowed." The third stage is "all clear," signaled by the falling sound of the siren. This means that the source of the attack was eliminated.

The "Anaconda" air base is an important logistical support hub for the entire theater of military operations in Iraq. It is a supply base on a dusty stretch about 50 miles northwest of Baghdad. Because of its importance, it is one of the most frequently attacked bases in Iraq.

Chapter 26

Hardships of the War

On October 18, I become sick with stomach problems and go to the military clinic. The doctor tells me that it is nothing serious. Apparently, I either took too many stomach pills and my body had a reaction to them, or the problems were caused by the stress that I have been under lately.

On October 19, I am still sick. I try to go to work as usual in the morning, but I have to go back to my place. I am feeling awful. It is especially difficult to be sick in these conditions. Before we arrived in Iraq, all of us received certain immunizations--about 10 or 11 shots for possible diseases. Meanwhile, I have continued to take malaria pills, which were recommended for every soldier and contractor in Iraq. Nevertheless, despite preventive measures taken by the U.S. Army, there are many potential dangers, stemming from poor sanitation and various insects (like flies and mosquitoes), which are especially prevalent in the summer. For example, "sand flies" can cause illness from just one bite.

Throughout my entire one-year assignment in Iraq, I tried to follow instructions, such as shaking out my bedding, boots, and clothing before using them, as well as placing a mosquito net above my bed while sleeping, particularly in the summer. This last recommendation was probably life-saving.

The room in which I am sleeping is an old one with many holes in it. It is part of a barracks from Saddam Hussein's army. Yesterday, I woke up in the middle of the night with a feeling that somebody was looking at me. I opened my eyes and saw a medium-size spider right above me; it was looking directly at me. The only thing separating us was the thin netting, and for several seconds we silently looked at each other. Finally, I moved my body and the spider ran away into one of the holes in the room. At that moment, I could imagine how the situation would have been if I didn't use the mosquito net; the spider might have been right on my face while I was asleep. Also, there are many deadly snakes in the Iraqi desert. The local Iraqis have warned me about "Black snakes." They say that their bites make you especially sick.

There is an area where Saddam Hussein's army planes were stockpiled after the invasion. They are mainly former Soviet MIG-type aircrafts, which were provided to Saddam's army. We go there with Sergeant R. When we arrive, the U.S. military police warn us that we should not go inside because the planes are full of snakes. Indeed, we can see snake traces leading out from the planes.

Unclean water remains one of the main problems in Iraq. Because of this, many soldiers and contractors use the bottled water provided by the U.S. military when they brush their teeth.

Chapter 27

Cultural Differences and Other Problems Become a Challenge

On my way back, Colonel Z., the commander of the Civil Affairs units gives me a ride. We have an interesting conversation about the situation in Iraq. He says that there are huge cultural differences between the Americans and the Iraqis. The Iraqis traditionally are friendly and open. According to their customs, they would first offer tea, ask about your family and engage in conversation before starting to talk about business matters.

Americans are also open, but they usually like getting right to the point of an issue. It is obvious that, in order to succeed in a different cultural environment, you need to abide and adapt to it. In other words, you need to follow certain rules and regulations. In Col. Z.'s opinion, the closer Americans get to Iraqis the more problems will arise.

He also says that Ambassador Paul Bremmer made a mistake when he immediately disbanded the Iraqi Army and Police at the very beginning. Instead, he should have kept the majority of them and paid them salaries. As a result of those steps, a security vacuum was created; a new Iraqi Army and police force were not in place to provide security, and the old Army and police were disbanded. Moreover, many of the old Iraqi military and police likely joined the ranks of the insurgency, for either political or financial reasons.

I ask Col. Z. whether we are winning in Iraq or losing. He replies that it is not clear. He says that part of the problem is that many of our soldiers were not trained for this kind of a guerilla warfare insurgency. They were mainly trained to fight regular armies. He adds that we do not have enough troops on the ground. I also heard some of the U.S.

service members voice their opinion that the top U.S. generals are sometimes reluctant to ask the political leadership about matters that might be unpopular with the American public. Asking for additional troops to be sent to Iraq to provide security seems to be one of those unpopular decisions. The immediate concern of those generals might be their promotions; they are afraid of jeopardizing their next star. The generals have a lot of power.

One of those generals mentioned by the service members is the former top U.S. commander in Iraq, Gen. Ricardo Sanchez. Many believe that he was not giving the President an objective evaluation of the security situation which, in reality, required more troops on the ground.

In the course of our conversation, I ask Col. Z. about the mortar and rocket attacks that are causing casualties among the soldiers and contractors from time to time. I wonder whether it is possible to prevent those attacks, using the many technological resources we have. Col. Z. says that the former Iraqi leader took lands from surrounding villages during his time, and he made this territory his military base. That is why angry Iraqis have been shelling the base since that time. Col. Z. mentions another reason: a lack of troops to more carefully patrol the surrounding area.

Then we talk about the invasion of Afghanistan by the Soviets, and how it was one of the main factors that ultimately led to the demise of the former Soviet Union. At that time, the United States was supporting the Afghan insurgency against the Soviets. Can the Iraqi insurgency have the same kind of consequences for the United States?

In reply, Col. Z. says that the war is very costly–again, there are not enough troops and no clear exit strategy. For example, millions of dollars were spent for the expansion of the "Anaconda" air base in Balad and for other bases which, in his opinion, were not necessary. We are virtually creating a little America in Iraq. Instead, he says we were supposed to spend the money to train and pay new Iraqi Army and security forces, to help quickly rebuild old schools or build new ones, to create infrastructure and medical facilities and to help with other necessary projects. That would definitely be appreciated by the majority of the Iraqis, and it is this area where the hearts and minds of the Iraqi people could be won. Z. says that ultimately we will have to leave, because the Iraqis need to take responsibility for their own country. At present, we need mobile special operations forces to deal with the situation.

On October 20, I am still sick. It is difficult for me; sometimes I have to run to the bathroom several times in the middle of the night. It is about 10 minutes away, and it is dangerous, because I have no idea whether an alarm went off. In that case, a second round of the mortar or rocket attack can occur at any time.

Tonight, I feel very bad and I am taken to the hospital by Staff Sgt. G. and our local translator Salman. I didn't eat anything the whole day, and when I tried to eat some soup I almost lost consciousness. Salman came in to check on me and realized that I was really in a bad condition. Then he immediately called G., and together they took me to the hospital. There, the medical personnel made me wait for some time. G. was upset about it, and he said that their behavior was not professional. It was clear that I was not a priority for them.

Earlier today, I had a conversation with Salman about different issues related to the situation in Iraq. Salman is always supportive of our efforts. He is valuable to us when we go out on missions in the surrounding villages. He knows the nuances and the geography of the area well. That proved to be important in a combat situation. By nature he is smart and loyal. His English is quite fluent for an average Iraqi. Generally, he is an intelligent and pleasant young man. He lives with his family in Taji to the north of our area. Sometimes, when it is too dangerous on the road, he stays on base. Frequently, though, he is traveling back and forth between the base and his house when he comes to work. It is dangerous, and we are always worrying about him. Many Iraqi translators and other contractors working for the Americans are being killed, injured or kidnapped. Still, those that survive keep coming to work on the base and on patrols with the American and coalition forces. The main reason is to earn money to feed their families. Salman is a Sunni Muslim. He told me that, if the insurgents would try to kidnap him, he would not give in; he would kill himself first.

Salman says that the Americans make many mistakes, mainly because they misunderstand the local culture and customs. For example, he mentions the western city of Fallujah, which has become very anti-American and one of the hotbeds of the insurgency. Salman says that, at the beginning of the invasion, the city was quiet and friendly toward the American and coalition forces. After a few months, though, problems started to emerge. For example, he says that there was one instance, among many others, when American forces were on the roofs of houses in the city with their shirts taken off. They were taking a sun bath, as they might do somewhere in the U.S. Other soldiers were taking pictures of passing Iraqi women. In another incident, an American soldier searched an Iraqi woman, touching her body in front of her husband. All this was happening in front of their husbands, brothers and other relatives. Salman said that this was unacceptable in accordance with the Iraqi culture, especially taking into consideration that Fallujah is, traditionally, a religious and conservative Sunni town.

Another mistake was when a chief negotiator from Fallujah was recently arrested upon leaving the mosque after prayers. He was a representative of the Fallujah residents, trying to find a peaceful solution to the ongoing conflict with the American forces.

I ask Salman for his opinion on the information that American troops could be planning to take over the city by military force. He replies the American forces had enough military power to do that, but he did not believe that it would solve the problem.

Later, when the military action against Fallujah took place, Salman's opinion would prove to be correct. It is believed that Fallujah's capture led only to the spread of the insurgency all over the country, and fueled it even more.

That same day, I went to the military hospital. Dr. Michael Cooper listens carefully to my health problems and examines me. Then he gives me some pills to take for about one week or 10 days. He says that he thinks there is not anything serious, but we should wait to see whether the pills are going to help. If not, I should come back to see him again. Generally, hospitals in these conditions have limited technical and medical capabilities and I did not have high expectations for the level of care I would receive.

On October 21, I have a conversation with Hussein, who is a local Iraqi Shiite Muslim. He works in the military store PX-BX on the base. Hussein says that the situation in Iraq is bad. He also adds that Abu Musaib Az-Zarqawi does not exist. The person with that name who had ties with Al-Qaeda had been killed by the former regime of Saddam Hussein in 1988 in the north of Iraq. This is a problem, because one of the main demands of the Iraqi government and American forces to the city of Fallujah was to hand over Az-Zarqawi and his Tawhid and Jihad group members and other fighters who, in reality, were not there. Otherwise, as the city was warned, they would be taken by force.

Hussein says that the reason for the American and Israeli presence in Iraq is mainly because of the Iraqi oil. He continues his thoughts and says that during the September 11 events in the United States, there were no Jews or Americans who happened to be at work in New York's World Trade Center Towers. All of them took off prior to the events. He says that most of the victims were people from other countries. According to Hussein, the September 11 events were certainly planned by Washington and Tel-Aviv. I realized that his views reflect the thinking of the average Iraqi on the street. Hussein was formerly a farmer, and presently he works in the U.S. military store to earn money to feed his family. He has no other choice.

Chapter 28

Important Logistical Hub

As of October 22, I am at the Balad Southeast air base in Iraq. It was one of the many Iraqi Air Force installations created in the 1970s. It was heavily damaged during the First Gulf War, and it has never been restored to its previous condition since then. Coalition forces took over the facility during Operation Iraqi Freedom and began using it as an air base and later as an important logistical hub for the entire theater of operations in Iraq.

The U.S. Air Force retained the name Balad for the base. The Army, however, calls it Logistics Support Area "Anaconda," or LSA "Anaconda." About 25,000 service members and civilians are stationed here. LSA "Anaconda" is one of the most frequently attacked bases in Iraq, averaging two to three times a day. Since January, five U.S. soldiers and one civilian have died here from indirect fire, which is mainly mortar or rocket attacks on the base.

Unfortunately, casualties in the combat area are happening in different circumstances, both on and off the base. Today, the Titan manager tells me that three linguists were sent to Germany for treatment. One was injured when the shrapnel from an IED explosion struck his face. Another linguist in his mid-forties had a heart attack, apparently from excessive stress.

Chapter 29

Casual Days Amid the Violence

On October 23, I am still sick, but I feel a little better than before. My wife sent me a message, asking me to come back to the United States for a medical checkup. She is concerned about my health, and she already made an appointment with a doctor for November 5 at 10 a.m.

Things are not going well in Iraq. Another hostage, a British Iraqi-Irish citizen, was recently abducted by one of the Iraqi groups. She was a director of Care International, an international humanitarian organization in Iraq, and has spent 30 years working in the country. Video footage showed the hostage tearfully appealing to British Prime Minister Tony Blair to not relocate British troops from the South of Iraq to the Baghdad area (which was being planned at the time as a backup to the planned U.S. assault on Fallujah) and withdraw British forces from Iraq. Otherwise, she said in the video aired by the Qatar-based Al-Jazeera television network, these might be her last hours.

On October 24, I feel a little better. I am hungry, but I can't eat much. I am still keeping to a diet and taking medicine. Tomorrow I am planning to go to work.

On October 25, I feel much better, but still weak, probably because of the diet and medicine. Today was quiet: no mortar or rocket attacks.

On October 26, I still feel sick and weak. I am continuing to take the medicine that Dr. Michael Cooper from the hospital prescribed for me. It makes me weak and dizzy.

On October 27, I go to work at the military convoy staging area. I am inside the trailer-office when we here a noise outside. At that moment, we see that one of the contractors from Saudi Arabia is behaving strangely. Another contractor who came with him is trying to help with translation and he is talking to our soldiers and KBR contractors. Then he turns to me, trying to explain in Arabic that his friend is mentally sick from excessive stress that he encountered on the road some time ago. I pass these explanations on to ours soldiers, but they still believe that the contractor is under the influence of drugs. At some point, one of the soldiers grabs the contractor by the neck and, as he tries to move, the soldier attempts to strangle him harder, although the contractor's hands are already tied behind his back. Specialist A. and I react to the soldier's actions and tell him to stop. The soldier stops strangling the contractor, but continues to stand right behind him, carefully watching his moves. We suggest to the KBR employees and military police who arrive shortly that they provide necessary medical assistance to the contractor. Then the Saudi contractor and his friend are taken away to the medical clinic and then they are probably interrogated.

On October 28, I go to see Dr. Cooper at the hospital, because I am still feeling weak, and I have a painful ache all over my body. At the entrance to the hospital, I see a lot of blood leading all the way into the hospital. Dr. Cooper comes, after a while, and says that there was an emergency. A soldier had been shot. I don't ask for any further details, but it is clear that the soldier is badly wounded.

On October 29, one of the contractors-truck driver who was a part of a U.S. military convoy comes in and says that about two and a half months ago they were attacked by Iraqis on the road, and two Turkish drivers were stabbed and killed. Another one of the drivers managed to escape with the U.S. military. He says that only one truck out of four arrived at "Anaconda" air base, and he was authorized by his company to take it back to Turkey. I notice that his hands are shaking while he is talking. He has gray hair and sad eyes. It is obvious that the incident seriously affected his morale.

On October 30, researchers of the British medical journal "The Lancet" estimate that as many as 100,000 Iraqis—many of them women and children–died since the start of the U.S.-led invasion of Iraq in 2003. Researchers at Johns Hopkins University and Columbia University of the United States and Al-Mustansiriya University in Baghdad conducted the study, which was published on the Lancet's website.

On October 31, I am not recovering. It is very difficult. I realize that I need to have a medical check-up.

On November 1, I talk to my employer's manager in the Balad area of Iraq. T. says that I need to get a letter from my doctor in the military hospital with a recommendation for the medical check-up, if it is advised by the doctor. I go to the hospital to see Dr. Cooper. He is receptive as usual, and he says that I definitely need to be checked in Germany, because we waited about a month and, unfortunately, my health condition has not improved. He adds that the U.S. military has limited technical capabilities in Iraq, compared to what is available in the United States and Germany. The doctor says that, even if nothing serious is ultimately found, it will be good for my peace of mind. He gives me a letter of recommendation addressed to my manager, advising that I be checked in Germany.

I ask Dr. Cooper about the soldier who was wounded the last time I came in, when there was a lot of blood in front of the hospital. The doctor says that the young soldier was shot in the head and, unfortunately, didn't recover. So, another mother, sister, brother or wife loses a loved one. This is unfortunate; I witness another bitter reality of the war.

I return to the office and call my manager. He says that I need to bring him the original letter, along with all the papers I got from the hospital so far.

Chapter 30

U.S. Elections and the Bin Laden Factor

On November 2, the U.S. presidential election is held. We are waiting to see how the results are going to affect U.S. policy in Iraq and the Middle East.

I talk to a female KBR employee on the bus on my way back to work. She says that one male KBR employee was so stressed out that he was crying. According to her, he was about 20 years old, an African American who arrived in Iraq about two weeks ago. So far, he could not adapt, was panicking and wanted to leave and go back home.

On November 3, preliminary results of the U.S. presidential elections indicate that President Bush will most likely be reelected for another four years. We talk with Maj. B. and Sgt. D. about the situation in Iraq. They consider our presence in Iraq to be generally justified, because Saddam Hussein did not allow U.N. inspectors to check the Iraqi military sites. Sgt. D., though, says she doesn't understand why the U.S. and coalition forces invaded Iraq, if the main reason was Al-Qaeda and its network.

In the meantime, a full transcript of Osama Bin Laden's recent video broadcast is made available. Bin Laden says that each dollar that Al-Qaeda spends on strikes has cost the United States one million dollars in economic fallout.

Bin Laden credits the "holy warriors" that he fought with against the Soviets in Afghanistan two decades ago with having "bled Russia for 10 years, until it went bankrupt and was forced to withdraw in defeat… So we are continuing this policy of bleeding America to the point of bankruptcy."

According to Bin Laden, Al-Qaeda is winning the war against the United States. The U.S. defense contractors linked to President

Bush, like the Halliburton Company, are also benefiting, while the American people and the American economy are losing.

Bin Laden says that the size of the economic deficit has reached record numbers, at more than one trillion dollars. In reality, the total national debt is near $7.4 trillion.

The fact is that it was not only the "holy warriors" in Afghanistan who brought about the collapse of the Soviet Union. There were internal political and economic problems in the Soviet Union. In addition, the U.S. support of the Afghan fighters ultimately contributed to the demise of the former USSR.

On November 4, I feel better. My manager says that he will send my medical papers to the central office in Baghdad, and then we need to wait for a reply from them.

President Bush is reelected. Some think that it is better to choose who you know, rather than who you do not know. We have known President Bush for the past four years, but we do not know what kind of president Senator Kerry would be.

On November 5, I go to the legal office. There is still no information or reply in connection with my citizenship. Capt. D. says that if we don't hear anything in two to three weeks, they will try to write another letter. He also advised me to contact my district Congressman or Senator for help with my citizenship issue.

On November 6, I go to the dental office to get my teeth cleaned. At my next appointment, they will do simple fillings. They do not do artificial teeth, crowns and other more complex work on the base, because of the limited dental equipment. The dentist is of German origin. He asks many of questions about the situation in Iraq, U.S. presidential election, etc. He thinks that the result of the U.S. presidential election proves that the conservative wing of the American population has prevailed, and that the majority Christian voters have a negative attitude toward Islam and Muslims. In his opinion, U.S. government experts on the Middle East should get a better understanding of the different economic, political, and cultural issues of the region. He suggests that they should go to the universities and other research centers to talk to the people who are knowledgeable on those issues.

My feeling is that he is unhappy with the ongoing situation in Iraq and the Middle East. He also says that the U.S. actions and policy in Iraq show that they were unprepared and uninformed. The dentist also talks about the Cold War era. He says that the former U.S. administration did not really tell the public what was going on in the former Soviet Union. Many people in the United States did not know that there were many of independent-minded people who did not want to be a part of the USSR.

Chapter 31

The Assault on Fallujah

Preparations are underway for a ground attack on the city of Fallujah. Reportedly, Fallujah is a stronghold of the Sunni Iraqi and international insurgency. Apparently the assault is imminent; it will happen sometime before the upcoming January elections in Iraq, but the order has to come from Interim Prime Minister Ayad Allawi. The Sunni Iraqi president hinted that the assault was not a good idea, because "further bleeding of the Iraqi people" is exactly what the insurgents want. Interim Prime Minister Allawi is a representative of the Shiite majority of Iraq, but he is considered to be a secular politician.

A Turkish truck driver comes in today. He was part of a U.S. military convoy two months ago. Their escort was attacked, and three Turkish truck drivers were shot and then beheaded by the insurgents. He had to transport their bodies back to Turkey. Now he is back in Iraq to pick up what is left of one of the trucks that was destroyed. Though the vehicle is almost completely destroyed and there is little left, his company gave him the legal authority to transport the remaining pieces of the truck.

On November 7, I am finally starting to get some days off after long periods of continuous work. We have several mortar attacks today. I don't have any information about casualties.

On November 8, I have been at the staging area for military convoys since the early morning. The assault on the insurgent stronghold of Fallujah has started. Between 10 and 15 thousand U.S. troops and about 2,000 Iraqi troops are taking part in the operations against the city, which is located to the west of Baghdad.

Some 26 Saudi clerics spoke out against the offensive. The influential Association of Sunni Scholars of Iraq said that the attack can create a backlash among the Sunni population of Iraq. According to the clerics, the insurgents in this situation have a legitimate right to resist the U.S. forces.

On November 9, we have had four mortar attacks and a rocket attack since 4:30 p.m. I am waiting in the bunker when the command post announces that all hospital personnel should report to the hospital. A mortar strike may have landed on or near the hospital or wounded U.S. service members may have been brought to the hospital from Fallujah. Everybody is expecting many casualties from the operation. Two soldiers who were standing next to me in the bunker say that there were a lot of wounded and killed already. We see military medical helicopters flying above us. The soldiers say that they were bringing dead or wounded service members from the Fallujah area. "Why did we have to make things worse?" said one of them.

On November 10, I heard that an Iranian reconnaissance plane flew above the U.S. "Anaconda" air base, an important U.S. logistical hub. Reportedly, it was flying at a low altitude and apparently taking pictures of the base. The United States warned the Iranians that, if it happens in the future, the planes would be shot down without notification. Today is a quiet day. We do not have any attacks. It is almost unusually quiet, and there is a strange feeling that something terrible is going to happen.

On November 11, the U.S. military operation in Fallujah is continuing. As of today, according to the military reports, the U.S. and Iraqi government troops took control of more than 70 percent of the city. Although there are small pockets of resistance throughout the city, the main insurgent forces have, most likely, fled prior to the beginning of the U.S. assault.

Today, Yasser Arafat, the president of the Palestinian Authority, died in a French military hospital after a long illness. This may seem unrelated to the situation in Iraq but, in reality, it is an event that has a certain significance for the entire Middle East region. His body will be flown to Cairo for a funeral ceremony that is being planned. Then he will be buried in Ramallah, outside of the compound where he spent the last three years of his life. The United States will be represented at the funeral by a high level delegation.

Meanwhile, in response to the Fallujah assault, several members of the interim Iraqi prime-minister's family have been kidnapped. Reportedly, the kidnappers threatened to behead them within 48 hours if their demands are not met.

We experience six mortar attacks tonight. According to rumors, one mortar shell killed two Indian workers and wounded six others at Dining Facility One.

On November 12, the military operation is continuing. According to the U.S. military, 23 U.S. service members have died and about 600 insurgents have been killed so far. Yesterday, one of the mortars landed 100 feet away from Specialist A., who is part of my military unit. The blast made him fall to the ground, but he was lucky to escape injury or death. It occurred close to the trailers where some soldiers, including A., live.

In another incident, one of the Turkish contractors became very sick. He had been sitting in the cabin of his truck without moving for three days. All of his body was covered with a wet, red rash. We call for the medics, who examine him and say that he might have a skin infection, possibly from an insect bite. We send him back to Turkey with another driver, because regulations say that the U.S. military cannot provide medical assistance on the base to foreign contractors unless there is a life threatening situation.

November 13 is the latest day of the continuing Fallujah military operation. According to the local Iraqis, the fighting is concentrated at the outskirts of the city. U.S. marines are trying to take control of the main positions around and inside of the city.

According to U.S. Army Maj. Richard Spiegel, the spokesman for the Thirteenth Corps Support Command, 10 contractors were injured Thursday evening as the result of a mortar or rocket attack by insurgents from outside of the "Anaconda" base. The building was hit at 8:34 p.m. at a time when 10 persons were working inside of it.

November 14 is a day off for me. We experience only two mortar attacks.

On November 15, the U.S. military operation continues in Fallujah. According to the U.S. military, 24 U.S. marines and more than 1,000 insurgents have been killed so far. More than 200 U.S. troops have been wounded. Starting three days ago, the wounded U.S. service members are mainly being sent to Germany, keeping the Landstuhl Regional Medical Center there busy.

The author in the Soviet Army: 1974-1976

The author is deployed to Iraq with the U.S. Army: 2004-2005.

Dr. Mahir Ibrahimov talks with children in a local village during a mission to open two water treatment plants in Balad, Iraq.

(Photo courtesy of 28th Public Affairs Detachment)

The author during a book signing ceremony for one of his books.

Historical sites and architecture in Iraq.

Chapter 32

Possible Implications of the Fallujah Military Operation

As of November 16, Fallujah is almost taken, but it is still not clear how that is going to affect the rest of the insurgency in Iraq. Before the U.S. assault there, the influential Association of Muslim Scholars of Iraq condemned the action. The Saudi Muslim scholars issued a fatwa, a religious regulation, against the attack. They suggested that, in case of such an attack, an Iraqi resistance against the U.S. forces would be legitimate. After the U.S. military operation began, the Islamic Party of Iraq announced in protest that it was withdrawing from the political process in Iraq.

The U.S. attack against the city has prompted insurgent violence across Iraq. The prediction that the capture of the city would simply scatter insurgents to other parts of the country seems to have proved correct. The U.S. military victory in Fallujah did not cause doubt in anybody's mind. The real question is what kind of political and security impact it will have in the future. The only immediate result is that the stronghold of the Iraqi and international insurgency has finally been taken. This area has been a "no-go zone" for a long time. Everyone remembers the horrific pictures of the U.S. security contractors who were captured and mutilated by insurgents amidst the cheering crowd of Iraqis. After that, the U.S. military started to plan an operation there. It was becoming clear that something had to be done with the city, which had become a symbol of the Iraqi resistance and the coalition forces' weakness. Although most of the predominantly foreign insurgent forces had left before the assault, fighting between the mainly local Iraqi insurgents and U.S. troops was intense.

World news agencies broadcasted incidents in Fallujah, such as one in which a group of U.S. marines entered a mosque and found several wounded and dead insurgents.

Pointing to one of the injured insurgents, a marine said, "He is still breathing." Another U.S. marine instantly pulled out his gun and shot the wounded man, saying, "He is dead now." This particular episode was aired today on Aaron Brown's TV news program.

We experienced two mortar attacks today. One landed on the military convoy staging area and the other near the trailers that are close to Dining Facility Number 1.

On November 17, my unit discusses what we each consider to be our most important thing. Spec. E. says that sex is important to her. Sgt. M. says that family is his priority. For Maj. B., it is his relationship with God. Sgt. C. names health as being important to him. So, there are different opinions on some issues. We are different people, but we are united on one team with the same mission. I like working with these individuals, and we have good relationships that are based on mutual respect. I think that we have a really good team, because everybody knows his or her responsibilities. I am helping with language and advice on the political and cultural issues; they, as military professionals, are doing their job, and they are doing it well. This is one of many units with which I am working. I know that when this time in Iraq is over, I will remember these people throughout my life. Once upon a time, we were in a war together, and the hardships and danger that we faced each day brought us closer together. We are especially close in the Civil Affairs Unit, mostly because we have to go outside of the base, which exposes us to possible attacks each time. Of course, I will remember Col. Z., Maj. L., Sgt. R., interpreter Salman, and others. I will also clearly remember the smell of the villages and the friendly greetings of the Iraqis. My concern is that military operations, such as those in Fallujah, could deal lasting damage to the relationships which we are slowly but steadily building with the local Iraqis.

According to the Associated Press, as of November 15, at least 1,194 members of the U.S. military have died since the beginning of the Iraq War in March 2003. In the Fallujah operation alone, 320 U.S. service members were wounded in action during a week of fighting. Many of them will remain invalids for the rest of their lives.

Casualties and sicknesses among the contractors are common here. Today, another contractor comes into our office. He says that he is very sick and tries to touch everybody's hands to make them listen to him. It is normal in many Middle Eastern cultures to touch people, but many American soldiers don't like it. At one point, revealing that his body is covered with nasty red spots. Our men ask me to tell him to leave, but he keeps talking and touching everybody's hands, trying to get closer. One of the soldiers pulls his gun out and points it at him, demanding that he leave the office. Finally, he leaves. The contractor's body really looked terrible, and everybody was disgusted. We didn't know what kind of illness it might be. Maybe it was caused by an insect bite; we have witnessed such cases before. Or it could simply be a nasty skin disease.

Chapter 33

The Political Process in Washington and the Situation in Iraq

National Security Advisor Condoleezza Rice is going to be replacing Colin Powell as the U.S. Secretary of State. In the spring of 2003, Rice's widely-quoted suggestion for how Washington should treat opponents of the U.S. led invasion was, "Punish France, ignore Germany and forgive Russia." Trans-Atlantic ties have improved to a certain extent since this statement got out, but Rice's international reputation persists mainly because of her tough stance toward opponents of the Iraqi war.

As of November 19, at least 1,198 members of the U.S. military have died since the beginning of the Iraq war in March 2003. The U.S. military says that it is expanding its investigation into the fatal shooting of a wounded man by a marine in a Fallujah mosque over the weekend. "The investigation will look into whether other wounded men in the mosque were also shot and killed," said a military spokesman.

American and Iraqi authorities have been trying to stem outrage over the shootings among the Iraqis. The Sunni Arab community in Iraq and across the region was especially angry over the incidents, which received wide coverage in the mass media. According to Iraqi Prime-Minister Ayad Allawi's office, he was "very concerned by the incident."

On November 20, there is still a lot of coverage in the Iraqi and international press about the incident where a U.S. marine shot a wounded Iraqi in a Fallujah mosque. The U.S. marine leadership claims a major success "in breaking the backbone of the Iraqi insurgency," but international analysts, including experts at the Center for

Strategic and International Studies in Washington, D.C., are less optimistic. According to them, the marines have won militarily, but the insurgents have won politically, which, in the long term, might be a problem for the U.S. led coalition in Iraq. Some analysts are of the opinion that insurgents can now more easily justify recruiting new members.

Secondly, the events in Fallujah can lead to a further polarization among the Sunni population of Iraq. All these factors are not contributing to the future stability of the country.

On November 21, I have a day off. It has been seven months since I came to Iraq.

On November 22, the departure of Colin Powell from the post of U.S. Secretary of State is widely covered in the press. It is mentioned that he has been respected as a Chief of Staff and a statesman, not only in the United States, but internationally as well. Many people, including Iraqis, now think that the U.S. administration consists primarily of hardliners, including Vice-President Dick Cheney, Defense Secretary Donald Rumsfeld and Deputy Defense Secretary Paul Wolfowitz. Some people believe that there is no longer an impediment to the hardliners. They can now have their way in future decision making in the State Department and other government agencies.

General elections in Iraq are scheduled for January 30. According to U.S. and Iraqi officials, they will be held in all territories despite the ongoing violence, including the so-called "Sunni Triangle" area. This triangle primarily consists of Anbar Province, which includes such volatile cities as Fallujah, Ramadi and Samarra.

According to the U.S. military, they might need an additional four to five thousand troops to provide security during the elections. This can be achieved by prolonging the stay of some military units for two to three months.

On November 23, I talk with two truck drivers who are trying to join a military convoy to Kuwait; one is Egyptian, the other is a Palestinian from Jordan. They tell me that the situation in Iraq will not improve, even if the Iraqi general elections are held transparently and democratically, unless the coalition forces leave the country. In their opinion, a foreign occupation of Iraq is one of the main reasons for the violence. According to them, another factor is that a country like Iraq needs somebody like Saddam Hussein; otherwise, instability will persist. They believe that there is a lot of ethnic and religious diversity in the country: Arabs-Shiite and Sunni Muslims, Kurds-Sunnis, Ezids and Shiites, Christians and others.

According to the drivers, if Saddam were still sitting in the president today, all the problems would have stopped immediately. Additionally, the Palestinian says that the American forces often kill innocent civilians. He says that several months ago he saw an entire family consisting of a mother, father and two children, killed in a car by U.S. soldiers.

The Pentagon says that three U.S. marines who were wounded in action during the Fallujah offensive died over the weekend in the U.S. military hospital in Germany. It raised the U.S. military death toll in Iraq for November to at least 101. Since the March 2003 invasion of Iraq, the only other month in which U.S. deaths exceeded 100 was last April, when U.S. marines fought fierce battles in the cities of Fallujah and Ramadi, located to the west of Baghdad.

The announced deaths mean that the death toll for the Fallujah offensive has risen to at least 54. According to the Associated Press count as of November 21, at least 1,221 members of the U.S. military have died since the beginning of the war in March 2003.

On November 24, there is preliminary information that the number of Turkish tankers is decreasing, and the number of contractors from countries such as Syria, Pakistan, Jordan and Egypt will be gradually increasing. I have already noticed, over the last several days, that the U.S. military convoys in the staging areas consist mainly of contractors from those countries.

During our break today, I began talking with a few members of our unit about salaries in the Army and in the KBR company, which is a subsidiary of Halliburton. It was mentioned that an E-4 enlisted soldier gets $3,000 a month ($36,000 a year). A captain earns $8,000 a month ($96,000 a year). The difference between a captain and a major is about $800 a month. A KBR truck driver is paid $8,000 a month.

On November 25, we celebrate Thanksgiving. We are having a holiday dinner in the dining facility with turkey from 11 a.m. to 3 p.m. This is a nice bit of home brought here to Iraq.

Meanwhile, about 5,000 U.S., British and Iraqi government forces launch an offensive to the south of Baghdad. They are still trying to crush the Sunni insurgency prior to the January elections. At the same time, a top aide to radical Shiite cleric Muqtada As-Sadr accuses the Iraqi government of violating terms of the August agreement that ended an uprising by As-Sadr's followers in Najaf.

As Sadr's top political adviser, Ali Smeisim says that contrary to the promise in the August agreement not to arrest members of As-Sadr's movement–"The government started pursuing them, and their numbers in prisons have doubled."

Smeisim says that Iraqi police arrested 160 As-Sadr loyalists in Najaf four days ago. He also accuses the government of conspiring with two major Shiite parties, Dawa and The Supreme Council for the Islamic Revolution in Iraq, to marginalize the As-Sadr movement, and to prevent its political activities and speeches in mosques and other places of public gathering. Trouble from As-Sadr's supporters and his Mehdi Army militia would further complicate the security situation in the country prior to the January elections.

On November 26, the major political parties, including Prime-Minister Ayad Allawi's own party, request a 6-month postponement of the general elections in Iraq, which had been scheduled for January 30. Several reasons are cited for the postponement, including the security situation and snowfalls in some regions, which could make voting difficult.

As of November 27, according to the Defense Department, at least 1230 members of the U.S. military have died since the beginning of the Iraq war in March 2003.

During the period from **November 28 to December 6** I am very sick with stomach problems. It is difficult under these conditions, but I am trying to cope with it. I have practically stopped eating and drinking anything, except a little food in the mornings. I lose a lot of weight, and everybody notices that I am becoming thinner and thinner. My appearance has completely changed. I become weak and pale. Because of unusual and extremely strong pains, I believe that I have cancer, and I've started to think about what I need to do for my family before I die. I also think about seeing my elderly mother, who lives in Baku, Azerbaijan. Meanwhile, I am trying to work as much as I can, and I've even stopped going to the bunkers when we are under attack.

On December 6, I learn that I am getting a vacation to go back to the United States via Germany on December 15. The main reason is to get a medical checkup because of my stomach problems.

The weekend was very bloody. Several U.S. service members, Iraqi National guardsmen and pro-government Kurdish militiamen were killed and injured. According to the Defense Department, as of today at least 1,265 members of the U.S. military have died since March 2003.

The weekend attacks showed that after the Fallujah assault the insurgency is still very capable of coordinating attacks and is eager to disrupt the general elections scheduled for January 30, 2005. The attacks are continuing to be directed against U.S. service members, Iraqi National Guard and security forces cooperating with the U.S. military.

A relatively new element has been observed lately; insurgents have started attacking pro-government Kurdish militiamen. They seem to be trying to involve Kurds in the ongoing violence and eventually civil war. So far, the Kurdish areas in the North are relatively calm and effectively controlled by the Kurdish Peshmerga militiamen.

Most of the attacks occurred in the Mosul area. There were also major attacks at the checkpoint leading to the heavily fortified Green Zone, which houses most of the foreign embassies and Iraqi Interim government. In an American forward operating base near Iraq's border with Jordan, a suicide car bomb killed at least two U.S. service members. Four slain men in Iraqi National Guards uniforms were found in north-western Iraq in the city of Tal Afar, which brought the number of bodies discovered in and around that town to at least seventy since November 18.

Additionally, the police in the northern city of Samarra came under attack Saturday. Mortars were fired at a station after midnight, wounding two officers. Gunmen injured two policemen in another attack at about 10 a.m., according to police Major Sadoon Ahmed Matroud. These are most violent areas at this time.

In the meantime, according to General John Abizaid, head of U.S. Central Command, the United States will boost its forces in Iraq to a record number of one hundred fifty thousand in coming weeks. This is because inexperienced Iraqi troops cannot ensure security on their own for the next month's national elections.

The increase will be made possible by extending the tours of duty of more than ten thousand soldiers and marines originally scheduled to return home in January. Their tours will be extended until March.

Assessing the security situation in the country, general Abizaid said that, "Things are better now than they were a month ago, but things are still not good enough". According to him, "While the Iraqi troops are larger in number than they used to be, those forces still have to be trained more. So, it is necessary to bring more American forces".

The number of one hundred fifty thousand U.S. troops is going to slightly exceed the number of American troops which had originally invaded Iraq back in March 2003.

Chapter 34

Vulnerability of Iraqi Security Forces and the Political Process in the Country

December 7. Jordanian born Abu Musaib Az-Zarqawi's group, Al-Qaida in Iraq, formerly known as Tawhid and Jihad, claimed responsibility for several of the attacks on Friday and Saturday.

On Sunday, another militant group, Jeish Muhammed ("Army of Muhammed" in Arabic), issued a statement saying that its fighters were planning more attacks against U.S. forces. The statement also warned Iraqis against aiding or cooperating with coalition forces, or else they would be attacked with a fury similar to that which is directed at U.S. forces.

Although the U.S. military had hoped that the Fallujah assault would cripple the insurgency, this bloody week has only scattered the rebels. In fact, after a brief lull, they resumed their attacks. The U.S.'s plan to make Iraq's army and police force play a more important role in the security of the country is not yet materializing. Instead, the Iraqi troops and security forces have only shown how vulnerable they are to decisive, devastating, and extremely demoralizing insurgent attacks.

The insurgents begin a new series of tactics, which include storming Iraqi National Guard posts and police stations to loot for arms and ammunitions. This is probably to compensate for what was lost in Fallujah and Samarra, where the U.S. military found and destroyed big caches of weapons. And, of course, one of the main purposes of the insurgency seems to be disrupting the upcoming Iraqi elections by creating an environment of fear and instability.

At the same time, about forty small political parties--mostly Sunni--meet on Sunday to demand that the upcoming elections be postponed by six months. But, President Bush, Iraqi Prime Minister Shiite Ayad Allawi, and Iraq's Sunni President Ghazi Al-Yawer, have stated that the vote will be held as scheduled.

In the meantime, for the first time, the U.N. special envoy to Iraq, Lakhdar Brahimi, bluntly states, "It is a mess in Iraq." According to a report from Reuters, when asked if it would be possible to hold elections under the current conditions, Brahimi said, "If the circumstances stay as they are, I don't think so."

It was the first time that a representative of an international organization has publicly raised a doubt in connection with the difficulty of going forward with elections. Also, the United Nations has been under intense pressure from Washington to accelerate its election preparations. Of course, the U.N.'s involvement would give a great degree of legitimacy to the Iraqi electoral process. But, in an interview with *The Los Angeles Times* last month, U.N. General Secretary Kofi Annan said, "[I will] not shrink from telling the Iraqi government if he thought the January polls were not feasible, although it would be up to the Iraqi government to decide whether to hold them. As we go, we will give them honest advice".

December 8. According to a classified cable sent by the CIA's station chief in Baghdad, cited by *The New York Times*, "The situation in Iraq is deteriorating and may not rebound any time soon." The cable warned that the security situation was likely to get worse, including more violence and sectarian clashes, unless there were immediate and decisive improvements on the part of the Iraqi government, in terms of its ability to assert authority and to build the economy.

According to officials who spoke with *The New York Times*, it looks like the security assessments, together with warnings from officials in Washington and on the ground, were more pessimistic than the optimistic picture being given by the Bush administration. The officials claim that the top U.S. military commander in Iraq, General George W. Casey Jr., reportedly reviewed the cable and initially offered no objections.

According to General John Abizaid, the commander of U.S. forces in the Persian Gulf region, "The U.S. forces in Iraq could start to be reshaped as early as next year, to reduce the number of combat U.S. troops and concentrate on the development of Iraqi security forces."

December 9. We had a very unpleasant incident in the military convoy staging area. Ahmed, a contractor-truck driver from Saudi Arabia, suddenly become very aggressive. Two soldiers and a KBR apprehended him, put him down on the ground and tied his legs and hands behind his back. A representative from PWC company said that he was drinking, but I managed to find out through their drivers that he had gotten mentally sick ten days ago, and that was when he started to behave strangely: tearing off his clothes, damaging other trucks, etc.

At one point, Ahmed tried to get up, although he was still tied together. Sergeant C. started to press his neck to keep him down. Specialist G. and I told C. to stop it.

I helped the KBR security and military police explain to Ahmed that nobody was going to harm him, and that he was going to be taken to the medical clinic to be helped. He calmed down and left with his cousin, military police, and KBR security.

But, the next day, I was told that he came back to the Management Control Team office at the military convoy staging area and was behaving aggressively again. At that point, one of the U.S. military police videotaped the whole incident. Later, I learned that he was sent out of the base to the north.

I finally received my ticket itinerary. I am supposed to be ready on Monday morning to leave by military plane for Frankfurt.

On December 1, I will fly from Frankfurt to Dulles International Airport by a civilian plane. Everything seems to be definite at this point. The main purpose is to do a medical checkup. I have already been given all of the necessary papers for short-term disability, in case it is something serious.

December 10. According to the Pentagon, the number of U.S. combat deaths in Operation Iraqi Freedom is now above 1,000.

On Tuesday, an American soldier was slain by small arms fire while on patrol in Baghdad, which brought the total number of U.S. combat fatalities to 1,001.

In the meantime, a 26-year-old American soldier, Private First Class H., was reportedly granted refugee status in Canada, after refusing to serve in Iraq. He told the immigration officials that the Army was drilling its soldiers to think of all Arabs and Muslims as potential terrorists; "We were being told that it was a new kind of war, and that these were evil people who had to be dealt with." According to N., the war in Iraq is illegal and fighting in it would have made him a war criminal.

Today, I also learned that the information that I had received about the contractor from Saudi Arabia who behaved aggressively on December 9 turned out to be wrong.

Major B., the commander of the 570 transportation team told me that after Ahmed was taken to the hospital they conducted a test that showed that he was on drugs. So, his friends and cousin lied to us about his mental illness.

Chapter 35

Major L.:
A True Military Professional in My Team

Major L. is a deputy to G5, 13-th Coscom. He is going home after being in Iraq for almost one year. He told me that it was time to go home but he felt a little sad because there were still many things to do in Iraq.

Indeed, he and our commander, Colonel Z., contributed a great deal to the mission in Iraq and they helped the local Iraqis through several different projects. Back in the U.S. Major L. is a policeman and he loves his job. He is originally from England and he speaks with a slight British accent. He is very precise and accurate in what he does and says. This is really a kind of person who does more than talks. When I first met L. I did not like him. I thought that he was not very receptive and friendly. But later I realized that he was one of the most reliable people I have ever met in my life.

He was one of the first soldiers who helped me get adapted to the new conditions when I first arrived.

When I asked him if he would do anything differently if he had to come to Iraq again he replied that he would not. He thinks that they have accomplished a lot and it was very important to reach out to the ordinary Iraqi people. That is exactly what they have been trying to do during their entire mission in the country: to help local Iraqis with water purification projects, with building schools, with medical assistance, etc. L. believes that the country has great potential to become a rich and democratic country. But a country's wealth and money should belong to the majority of the people not just to a certain part of the population.

I ask L. about the upcoming elections, and he says that elections are an important part of the democratic process, and it will take several elections before a real democratic and free society is established in Iraq.

I then asked L. his opinion about the ongoing insurgency in the country.

He thinks that it is mainly local and the most uneducated Iraqis that are joining the insurgency. But foreign fighters are also coming in across the Iraqi borders, and they have political and religious agendas.

I was interested to know what L. learned during his mission in Iraq.

He said that most Iraqis want to live in peace, raise their children, and feed their families. They are really good people.

When I asked if our mission is going to ultimately succeed in Iraq, L. replied that he believed so, and the sooner the better. "What makes you believe that?" I asked him. He said that you have to believe that success is possible; otherwise we wouldn't come here in the first place.

I asked L. if he thought that Fallujah was a turning point in fighting insurgency.

He was not sure but he said that it seems more quite lately. Maybe because, as some believed, Fallujah was a safe haven for leadership of the insurgency from which attacks could be planned and coordinated.

But I reminded him that, according to the reports, most insurgents left Fallujah prior to the assault and scattered around the country.

L. thinks that not all of them could flee and many of them were killed.

We also talked about the involvement of foreign countries in the insurgency in Iraq.

Are any foreign states helping the insurgency in Iraq directly or indirectly?

He replied that, according to the news, they are involved but he doesn't have any knowledge or precise information about it.

L. is very much satisfied with the work they have done as a team in Iraq. According to him 85 different projects have been completed and $ 4.3 million have been spent so far. Several thousand Iraqis were employed. All these efforts were helping the Iraqi economy and improving infrastructure.

Particularly, such surrounding villages as: Abu-Hassan, Abu-Assi, Al-Hatemiya, Abu-Bali, Al-Faruz, Abu-Feizi, Al-Shehabi, Ar-Rafayeya and many others have been receiving consistent help from our unit through different projects. I have been in the majority of those villages, and we have been dealing with them through the Yastrib, Balad and Ad-Dujeyl city councils of the Salahaddin province.

L. also added that 24 water purification projects are currently being built in 24 villages.

L. said that generally it has been a great experience to be in Iraq at this important time. It has also been very difficult to be away from his family for so long. He thinks that you cannot always be involved in every important mission and event in the world. At some point you need to make your family a priority and take care of your children. L. mentioned that there are already some preliminary plans for their team to come back to Iraq, with a new mission, in just two years.

I will remember L. as an example of a good soldier and a real man who can be reliable in any situation.

December 11. Today we had a meeting in the Civil Affairs Unit, G5. There were more than ten sheiks and elders from different surrounding villages around the "Anaconda" air base. The main purpose of the meeting was to discuss financial issues related to different ongoing and upcoming projects.

Then we had a luncheon with tea and it was a good opportunity to communicate. Lieutenant Colonel K., the new G5-Civil Affairs Unit commander, who replaced Colonel Z., introduced himself. Colonel Z. and all his team are going back to the States due to the completion of their assignment in Iraq. Major L., who was leaving, and Major C., who was replacing him, were both present. A local interpreter and I were helping with cultural communication and interpreting.

It was a very productive and constructive meeting which lasted for several hours.

Chapter 36

January Elections

In the meantime, 228 candidates for the January 30 elections were announced. The candidates include independent Sunni Muslims, a Shiite Kurdish group, members of the Kurdish Yazidis minority religious sect, and a Turkomen movement. Also, the members of the Iraqi National Congress, led by former exile and one-time U.S.-backed Ahmed Chalabi, are included in the list of the candidates. The alliance of Shiites includes the major Shiite political parties: the Supreme Council for the Islamic Revolution in Iraq and The Islamic Dawa Party. Both parties have strong ties with Shiites but non-Arab Iran. Reportedly, representatives from Muqtada As-Sadr's movement refused to be included in the list, because they first wanted to see how the vote would go and what the results were going to be. Then, the group would make a decision about participation in the next stages of the elections.

According to As-Sadr's representative in Beirut, the movement intends to be careful in supporting the occupation. As-Sadr's movement is gaining support at a grassroots level, among the poor and young Shiite population of Iraq. In addition, As-Sadr's lack of participation in the elections makes the situation unpredictable; he has sent mixed messages in the past, as well.

So, the elections are supposed to choose a 275-member Assembly that will write a permanent constitution, which is supposed to be adopted in a referendum next year. This will then become a legal basis for another general election, scheduled by December 15, 2005.

Chapter 37

Sergeant S.

December 12. S. is another member of the G5-Civil Affairs Unit. He is always quite; he talks very little or not at all. He was like that when I first met him and he has been like that during his entire mission in Iraq. When it was time to prepare for the mission, he would quietly but very professionally prepare his weapon. First he cleans it, and then checks it several times. Because he is virtually on the front line of the mission, he is always sitting in the front seat of the military vehicle with his weapon loaded and ready in the case of attack. He is always ready to protect us all; not just himself.

But time has come for this young but already very experienced man to go back home. His mission is coming to an end.

Before his departure I wanted to talk to him about his impressions of Iraq.

I asked him how he felt about going home after being away for almost a year.

He said that he was very excited to get home as soon as possible, but unfortunately the process of getting home is slow because of different procedures and time difference.

I asked him if he would do anything differently if he was able to redo his mission from the beginning, and he replied that what he was doing here was very important and he wouldn't change anything. He thinks that the whole process of Civil Affairs, which involves rebuilding efforts and helping people, is the most important thing that the Army is doing in Iraq. He says that fighting is not our job, although we need to be ready to protect ourselves if necessary. Instead our main job should be to reach out and to help people with education, infrastructure and other projects in order to gain their trust.

I asked S. for his opinion about the upcoming elections.

He thinks that the elections are mainly about the Iraqi people's ability to run their own country, without the feeling that they need the U.S. to help them. He believes that we can't tell Iraqis how to run their country; the country must be entirely in their hands.

Some Iraqi politicians are of the opinion that the elections should be postponed because of the security situation. I asked S. what he thought of this. He replied that he didn't think that the elections should be postponed because the security situation will probably remain the same for some time. He thinks that the elections should be held on time.

I asked S. what he thought about the war in Iraq. Was it legitimate to invade Iraq even though the U.N. did not support the invasion of Iraq, no weapons of mass distraction were found, and there was no link found between the Saddam Hussein regime and Osama bin Laden?

S. replied that Saddam Hussein was overthrown in order to eliminate a potential threat against the U.S. and the U.S. had to stay to help the Iraqi people politically and economically.

I asked S. for his opinion on whether or not everything was going well in Iraq so far.

He said that yes, everything was going well. As an example he cited the area that our team was responsible for. A lot of things have already been accomplished here but he expressed a hope that, down the road, Iraqis would be able to handle their own affairs. He thinks this it will take some time.

"What about the insurgency? Is it a serious threat to the country as well as to the U.S. interests here?" I asked him.

S. considers the insurgency a serious threat. He is reminded of that every time when we go to the villages outside of the base. We need to be alert because we could be attacked at any moment. He thinks that although the percentage of Iraqis that are part of the insurgency is relatively small there is enough to cause a threat to the security of the country and to the U.S. interests in the region. He said it is still hard to tell exactly whether or not they can disrupt the upcoming elections because their potential is still unknown. In his opinion, if there is good security in place everything should be fine.

Did the Fallujah assault change the security situation in the country?

He thinks that Fallujah was a primary place where the insurgents were stationed and that is why he thinks that the Fallujah operation obviously broke the backbone of the Iraqi insurgency.

Is there support from abroad for the insurgency in Iraq?

S. thinks that there is no foreign involvement; it is primarily an Iraqi insurgency.

What does the insurgency want?

S. said that insurgents are suspicious of foreign countries. They fear that America wants to impose their culture and way of life onto the Iraqis. In this case a religion plays an important role.

December 13-14. I am still very sick. I am waiting to go back to the States for a medical checkup.

In the meantime the Civil Affairs G5 team has already left because their mission in Iraq was completed. The new rotation has already arrived.

My impression of the entire outgoing unit was very positive, especially in the case of commander Colonel Z. He is a very intelligent and nice person. I think the entire outgoing unit will find a special place in my heart for the rest of my life.

They really were very special, both as professionals and most importantly as personalities. We were a good team and we had a deep mutual respect for what each of us was doing in those difficult and dangerous conditions. They called me a multitalented interpreter; I called them good friends and excellent military professionals. We took pictures together and when I saw them off all of us wished to meet again in the future. You never know, maybe we will. But right now it is so sad that they depart.

Chapter 38

Vacation Time

December 15. I am leaving for vacation, so that I can have my medical checkup in the U.S. I am dressed in a military desert uniform, which made it clear that I was coming from Iraq. In the airport, many Americans approach me, thanking me for what I was doing for the country.

At the Frankfurt airport, I was approached by an aged American, his wife, and a military pilot who was also coming back from Iraq. The husband and wife were very grateful to us and said that they appreciated our service for the country.

On the plane, a young German woman with a child came up and tried to speak to me. She could barely speak English, and I don't speak German at all. But, I was somehow able to explain that I also had a daughter, and that I hadn't seen her for many months.

An older American man was sitting next to me. He told me that, although he didn't support the war in Iraq and the current U.S. administration, he did support our soldiers serving in Iraq.

My wife and my daughter were waiting for me at the Dullas International Airport. When I came out, they rushed to me and happily hugged me. They were carrying a balloon that read "Welcome Home." I saw how they missed me and realized how much I had also missed them. I managed to hide my teary eyes from them. We took a few pictures together before we left the airport.

The next several days were devoted to checking my stomach and spending time with my family. My doctor reiterated what the military hospital doctors said back in Iraq: I probably had a minor stomach infection or perhaps it was a result of the stress.

During the next few days, my family and I went to several restaurants. Then, we enjoyed Christmas and New Year's Eve at home, exchanging gifts and spending time together. We generally had a good time.

The last days of my vacation were spent looking for possible job options after the completion of my Iraq assignment, which should end in April or May. I have sent my resume to different government agencies, including the Department of Defense, the Defense Intelligence Agency, and other agencies and organizations.

I met with the head and other representatives of the Russian section of the State Department's Foreign Service Institute; I taught there before I went to Iraq. I was told to call sometime in February to inquire about possible vacancies. This is the most realistic job opportunity at this time. I also met with the heads of the Institute's Arabic section.

But, the most realistic opportunity for me is to teach in the Russian section, because the head of the section, U., and consultant P., said that they already knew me from my previous performance in their section.

When we met, they praised my service to the country. They were calling me a hero and were very kind to me. Teachers at the Institute were curious about Iraq and asked many questions about my service. They asked about the danger of the area, how the soldiers felt about the war, and about the culture, customs, and opinions of the Iraqis.

But, with the exception of a few people, like U. and P., nobody cared about the situation in Iraq and our troops there. Those who did care were mainly pessimistic about the upcoming Iraqi elections and the general situation in this country.

The general perception is that the insurgency in Iraq is getting stronger and more sophisticated. In fact, this opinion was confirmed by U.S. General Smith. I also saw an American documentary about the entire pre-war situation and September 11th. The main idea of the movie was that the Iraqi war completely devoted to the business and political interests of a few people, like former President George H.W. Bush, President George W. Bush, and former U.S. Secretary of

State James Baker, who had business relationships with the Saudi royal family.

During my vacation, we also visited my long-time friend K. and her husband L. P. is an editor of the *Washington International Magazine* and L. is a pilot. At P.'s house, we met L.'s son A., his wife M., and a friend of Patricia's who was "involved in working with projects related to Russia." All of them were very interested to listen to the notes that I had made about my Iraqi experience, especially A.. But, it seemed like all of them were pessimistic about the war in Iraq.

The next day, we invited P. and L. out to dinner. We had a nice time together. P. and L. said that I need to find a good job after the completion of my Iraq assignment and that they were going to work on my resume to make it more attractive for future job applications. They were also impressed by the two letters of recommendation that I had brought with me from my commanders in Iraq.

On January 3, my wife and daughter drove me to the airport. My vacation was coming to an end. Fortunately, I was healthy again and could go back to Iraq to continue my service. But, it was very difficult to leave my family again; and I saw how difficult it was for them, as well. My wife had tears in her eyes as she watched me kiss our daughter goodbye. My daughter, meanwhile, became very protective and held tight to me all the way to the airport. The previous day, she had given me a touching note that read, "Dad, be very careful. I love you very much. I would terribly hate to see you hurt. War is no joke, be serious and this cumbersome weight will soon be off your shoulders and hopefully with God's help you will come back home safe, the way you were when you left and better than before, mainly alive! Remember most importantly that I love you very much. You are the best!" That was my 13 year-old daughter's farewell note.

After my family left, I was waiting for my flight inside of the terminal when L. unexpectedly came up to me, dressed in his pilot uniform. He was also flying that day; he would be piloting a plane to Munich. He knew that I was scheduled to leave, and he came to see me and to say goodbye. We had a nice conversation. He asked me to be careful in Iraq and told me that his son A. was impressed with me and admired what I was doing. L. told me that A. found his work as a radiology doctor to be very boring.

Chapter 39

Going Back to Iraq

On January 4th, I arrived at Frankfurt and the next day, as scheduled, we boarded a military plane heading to Balad, Iraq. I am writing this chapter while on the plane. It is approximately a four-hour flight.

During the flight, the plane frequently shook and the pilots asked us from time to time to fasten our seatbelts.

Across from me on the other side there seems to be an Iraqi government official, maybe a minister. Next to him a young woman, possibly his daughter and several body guards. They look like Americans. Next to them, there is a blonde woman. I can clearly hear her speech; she is an American, probably an assistant to the Iraqi official or a friend of his.

I took some pictures while flying. Next to me is a female American soldier who looks very tired. She is sleeping now.

We are getting closer to the country. I got hungry and had some snacks: some sandwiches, juice, conserved fruits, raisons, etc. Then I slept. I was very tired when I boarded the plane. My colleague, who is flying with me to Iraq, is also coming back from vacation. He is originally an Iraqi Kurd and is now waiting to get his U.S. citizenship to bring his wife from the north of Iraq to the U.S. In the U.S. he lives in Virginia.

According to him, before the elections, "Nobody knew what might happen in Iraq." He goes off the base to Baghdad almost every day. He patrols the streets of the city with the military police and he says that his job is very dangerous. He said that as soon as he gets his citizenship he and his Iraqi wife will move to the States immediately. Generally he thinks that one year in Iraq is quite reasonable but not more than that because of the danger and because you must be away from your family. He said that the longer you are in Iraq the more likely you are to get hurt.

We landed at the U.S. "Anaconda" air base on time as scheduled. Immediately, the important Iraqi official and his entourage were surrounded by the athletically built U.S. security guards and quickly taken away in the cars which were waiting right where the plane landed.

A representative of the Titan National Security Solutions Corporation was waiting for me and my colleague. After we received our baggage, we were driven to our locations. A group of five or six linguists were heading to Baghdad and one person, a Kurdish American was going to the north of the country.

The whole next day I was sleeping because I was exhausted. Then I cleaned up my room. This is a desert area and while I was away the room became very dusty.

January 7. I went to the medical clinic to check my blood level and for malaria pills which all of us were taking so far. After those pills we needed to take a new medicine to clean up the liver. Then I went to work.

Everybody in the Civil Affairs Unit and at the military convoy staging area was happy to see me again. I realized how they appreciated my work.

At the military convoy staging area soldiers are leaving on January 24 due to the rotation. They are going back to the U.S., through Kuwait. Three soldiers are temporarily replacing them and then seven soldiers will permanently come to the post.

Commanders of my military units, Lieutenant Colonel K. and Major B., talked with me in length about how I spent my vacation and how everything was going in Iraq. They repeatedly said that they were very glad to see me again.

Chapter 40

Back to Work Amid Continuing Violence

Today a car bomb exploded outside a police academy south of Baghdad during a graduation ceremony. At least twenty people were killed as a result. According to the Iraqi Interior Ministry figures the number of Iraqi policemen killed in the last four months of 2004 was at least 1,300.

Also most notably among the recently killed were Baghdad governor Ali Al-Haidari. He was killed on Tuesday and was known for his close cooperation with the U.S. troops.

The insurgency activity is expected to increase prior to the Iraqi elections. But according to the top U.S. military officials such as Major General Peter Chiarelli, commander of the multinational division in Baghdad: "U.S. military officials expect the security situation to be better by January 30", at least in Baghdad.

In the meantime according to an Associated Press count as of Tuesday at least 1,336 members of the U.S. military have died since the beginning of the Iraq war in March, 2003.

According to Iraq's intelligence chief Major General Mohammed Abdullah Al-Shahmani in his interview for the pan-Arab newspaper Ash-Sharq Al-Awsat between 20,000 and 30,000 insurgents are operating throughout the territory of Iraq. They are led by Syria based former regime leaders and Baath party members and getting moral support from about 200,000 people in Iraq mainly in the Sunni areas. He particularly mentioned the name of the former leading Baathist Mohammed Younis Al-Ahmed and Sabaawi Al-Hassan, a half- brother of Saddam Hussein. According to the intelligence chief they are in Syria and they are providing financial support to the insurgents in Iraq.

January 8. I went to work to the military convoy staging area. Major P. from my Unit is preparing to leave very soon due to the new rotation. But he is very unhappy with the evaluation he received. He says that it is mainly based on his performance while he was in Kuwait, but not in Iraq. And because it is negative, it can affect his future promotions as an Army reservist.

Later today, the Civil Affairs Unit went on a mission to a nearby village. I didn't go this time, because I was very tired after the trip back to Iraq. Although I promised my wife that I would not leave the base, I do plan on continuing to go out to the villages. For me, the danger is an interesting challenge and an opportunity to see and experience the indigenous and unique Iraqi cultural spirit, which can be felt only in the villages. I like the environment of the Iraqi rural areas, particularly the smell; it reminds me of Azerbaijan, Russia, Baltic republics, and other places that I have been to in the past. Villages are, in my opinion, a real reflection of the peoples' culture and customs.

I remember one time when I was a young soldier training in the Soviet Army. It was a harsh winter and our unit was located up on a hill. Down the hill, there were Russian villages along the Akhtuba River, a branch of the Volga River that stretched through the vast territory. I had been sick with a fever for several days and could not recover. I was very thirsty and needed medicine. But, nobody wanted to help me in those brutal conditions, especially since I was a young soldier. At the time, the ugly "dedovshchina system," in which the commanding soldiers mistreated the young soldiers, was very common in every Soviet military unit at the time. One night, I put something under my blanket to make it look like I was sleeping in my bed. Then, I left the unit under the cover of the night and went down the hill to the village. I remember that when I got to the village, dogs everywhere started to bark. I was passing one house after another and finally I decided to knock on one of the doors.

At one point, I got scared of what I was doing and wanted to run away. But, it was too late: an elderly man had opened a door. He looked surprised and asked me, " How can we help you, son?" This area was particularly respectful towards the service members. He saw my uniform and immediately realized that I was a member of the military unit from up on the hill.

I explained that I was very sick and needed help, but that the home care that I wanted was impossible to get, since my home was very far away. He immediately said, "Come inside, son. It is cold outside." I went in the house and saw that his family was already up: the man's wife (a nice elderly woman), their daughter, and their granddaughter. The man explained to his family who I was and why I was there. I immediately felt their friendliness and warmth. They placed me beside the fireplace and brought me hot "shee" (Russian soup) and tea. They took my temperature and it was very high. They were surprised by how I continued to exercise and fulfill my daily duties, in spite of being so sick in such cold weather. Almost every day, we ran up and down the hill with full ammunition, sometimes even entering the freezing water of the river as a part of the training. They gave me some medicine to reduce the fever. While I was drinking hot tea and eating, the entire family was sitting around the table and looking at me. Their eyes were full of understanding and sympathy. They did not ask me any questions until I had finished my shee and tea, and regained some strength. I told them about myself, my family back in Azerbaijan, and about the fight that I had had with the sergeant, when he hit me for not reason.

I learned from them that the couple's daughter had made a mistake in marrying. Soon after they wed, her husband began drinking heavily and beating his wife. By that point, they already had already had their daughter. One day, they got fed and asked him to leave. Since then, they had been living together as one family. I felt so sorry for them, because they were all such kind and generous people. After several hours of getting to know one another, they gave me a nickname: "black-eyed pretty young man." That snowy night, listening to the sound of barking dogs and getting to know wonderful people, will be in my mind for the rest of my life. I was drinking one cup of hot tea after another, talking to them, having a good time. And I couldn't imagine that a time would come many years later when I would be in another village somewhere in the Middle East, but with a completely different environment and culture. We didn't even notice when it was 5 a.m. and people started to rise at cockcrow. I said that I needed to go, to make sure that I could get back to the unit unnoticed. The family was worried about me and offered to go to the unit to talk to my commanders, in order to protect me. But I was young and proud. I didn't want to disturb them. I assured the family that I could handle things myself and everything was going to be O.K.

They asked me to promise them that I would come to see them again. I did, because I honestly wanted to see them again. The entire family--which had not gotten any sleep that night because of me--was standing in the doorway seeing me off. All of them hugged me, and I left with the elderly man. He saw me off until the end of the village and said that if they didn't hear from me, they would come to the unit looking for me. He gave me some food that his wife had prepared for me.

My entire unit was up waiting for me when I returned.

When I was leaving for the village, somebody had spotted me and informed the commanders. Although I was swiftly punished, I never regretted my brief escape, because I met those wonderful people. During my six month tenure, I managed to see them numerous times. But, after the completion of my training, I was sent to the Baltic region for the rest of my service and I never saw them after that. I remember how their friendly eyes made me feel like I was home. They had also hinted that they wanted me to become part of their family, because their granddaughter was about my age.

I was stationed for a year and a half in the vast Kaliningrad oblast (formerly Kenigsberg of Eastern Prussia, a part of Germany). This area is also full of interesting villages, with a wonderful natural setting and a fascinating culture. Their area is made up of many Germans,

Latvians, and Lithuanians living amongst the Russians.

I also enjoyed going to those villages and meeting different people. The territory is huge, and I could sometimes see half-ruined houses that had not been lived in for years, complete with yards full of untouched apple trees. They had probably belonged to some German Herzogs who lived in this area before the Soviets took over.

It was many years ago. Now I am in Iraq. Everything is different here. The main difference is that I am in the war. And this is an unpleasant reality.

January 9. I came to the dining facility to have some lunch. I met Sergeant First Class R., who is with the supply detachment at the "Anaconda" air base in Balad. He served during the Vietnam War, the first Gulf War, and is now serving in the second Gulf War in Iraq. He is 54 years-old and says that this will probably be his last overseas deployment.

I told him about the incident the previous day, when an officer from the mayor's office on the base told me--very roughly--that I should wear my ID around my neck. He was right about it, because I forgot to do it that day. But the way he talked to me was not very pleasant.

Sergeant R. said that I shouldn't pay attention to these kinds of incidents, because many soldiers are very stressed. Some of them lost friends during combat and being away from family is adding to the stress. According to R., there was an incident at the U.S. base "Morez" in the city of Mosul that resulted in tightened security; reportedly, about twenty American soldiers were killed by a suicide bomber. Several new security measures were enforced: additional security guards at the fronts of the dining facilities, no bags allowed anymore, no third country nationals, and local hired Iraqis are allowed to enter the dining facilities anymore. R. told me in confidence that there have been attempts to throw some explosives into the dining facilities on the "Anaconda" air base. But, the attempts were prevented. He hopes that the January 30th elections will help to improve the security situation. He also thinks that Iraq is a very ancient country and deserves to be rich.

In the evening, we have a joint dinner with Lieutenant Colonel K.--a new commander of the Civil Affairs Unit-- and his deputy, Major C. K. said, "We are not leaving here," meaning that the U.S. troops will stay in Iraq, in any case. According to him, insurgency will always be present in Iraq, like in Palestine. He also said that the Iraqi elections are very important. Then, he asked questions about my background, my professional interests, and how my book is coming along.

Colonel K. has already been in many overseas deployments before: Bosnia, Kuwait, Korea, and now Iraq.

January 10. We have an incident with a young Iraqi man. Military police is picking me up to help resolve the incident.

The local Iraqi was trying to carry a compass inside of his wallet onto the base. But, the security at the gate found it out. Now, the military police are trying to find out why he was trying to take the compass on the base. I am interpreting for the Iraqi. He says that he didn't know that he couldn't take compass inside of the base, and that he never even used it on the base.

After we talked to the Iraqi man, he was taken away--probably for further interrogation. A military policeman told me that he could use the compass to direct the insurgents where to shell the mortars and rockets onto the base. Also, another policeman said that the man was trying to hide his hands, apparently trying to keep the compass hidden, as well. In my opinion, the military police actions were justified in taking the necessary security precautions; our safety could depend on this.

In the meantime, the pre-election violence is continuing. The U.S. is trying to negotiate with the leaders of the Sunni minority in Iraq to participate in the elections. At a meeting on Saturday, members of the powerful Association of Muslim Scholars reportedly relayed their request to a senior U.S. embassy official that the group will abandon its call for a boycott of the elections if the United States gives a timetable for withdrawing multinational forces from Iraq.

In the meantime, as an indication of the continuing violence, seven Ukrainians and one Kazakh, who were serving as part of the coalition in Iraq, were killed Sunday in an explosion. According to the military officials, they were loading bombs that could be used by warplanes.

January 11. I am trying to find out about my tax issues. We have tax exempt status, and I am trying to find out what percentage of the paid taxes will be returned to me after the completion of my deployment in Iraq.

January 12. I manage to find out that I am supposed to be out of the U.S. for 330 days to be able to get my taxes back, and I cannot be in the United States for more than 35 days. I can be in the U.S., but I will have to pay social security taxes and Medicare, as usual. It looks like only federal taxes will be returned.

A contractor- truck driver came in. His truck broke down near Taji. After his truck broke down, the military convoy left, and the contractor got a ride with another driver to the base. Because of security reasons, convoy can never wait on the road--they always need to be moving.

We contacted the military management control team in Taji to recover his truck. But, experience tells us that his truck was most likely taken away by local Iraqis or burned down by insurgents.

Chapter 41

Political Process Amid the Violence

In the meantime, Interim Prime Minister Ayad Allawi says, on Tuesday, that some areas of Iraq will probably be too unsafe to take part in the January 30th elections. This is his first public acknowledgement by the Iraqi interim government that they would not be able to secure those areas controlled by insurgents. Indeed, the country's volatile Anbar province, which includes Ramadi, Fallujah and Samarra to the west of Baghdad, and areas in the north around Mosul have seen little preparation for the elections so far. Violence in the other parts of Iraq is also ongoing.

The attacks are mainly aimed at Iraqi police, security forces and the U.S. led coalition. In one instance, a suicide car bomber targeted the police headquarters in Tikrit, which killed six people and wounded twelve.

Our local Iraqi translator, Salman, says that many people in the villages in his area of residence are afraid to go to the polling stations because of the security risks, and these are mostly Sunni areas. The area around "Anaconda" air base, where we are stationed, has a mixed population of Sunnis and Shiites. These are the villages near the city of Balad.

January 13. Three trucks which were part of U.S. military convoy are involved in an accident near the U.S. base in Taji. When a first truck had to stop quickly as a result of the accident, it was hit by a second truck from behind, which in turn was hit by a third truck in the convoy. We gave an incident report to one of the drivers to present to his employer.

We are driving with Sergeant M. in a military vehicle. He says that after the events of September 11 we should have come to Iraq and hit five times harder than we were hit and then to leave, rather than stay and try to help them rebuild. He says that it is not possible to defeat all terrorists and insurgents but in his opinion the U.S. is going to have to stay in Iraq for a long time. Due to the troop rotation, Sergeant M. and his team are supposed to leave Iraq soon but there is speculation that if they don't leave by January 24, their stay will be extended.

According to M., we have only 12,000-14,000 troops and other personal on "Anaconda" air base out of 150,000 over the entire country, and if the Iraqi National Guard, being trained by the U.S., decides to turn against us, they can very easily overrun us.

January 14. I am in the office at the military convoy staging area. A wounded truck driver-contractor came in. His convoy was attacked by the insurgents. While we are making calls to locate a doctor he unexpectedly collapses in front of us. Obviously the loss of blood and the stress have significantly weakened him. We are trying to help him as much as we can.

January 15. The father of a truck driver comes in. His son was injured in both his legs when his military convoy was hit by an IED (improvised explosive device) while on the way from "Anaconda" to the designated destination point. He was taken by a U.S. helicopter to the hospital on the base. After he recovered he was sent back home to Turkey. His father is trying to recover his truck and take it with him but the task is difficult because the attack occurred near the Samarra city bridge where there is a lot of insurgent activity. The U.S. military agreed to try to recover the truck but the result is unlikely going to be positive due to our previous experiences. The truck is probably not there anymore and it is very risky for the troops.

In the meantime, violence seems to be on the rise prior to the January elections. One of the latest victims of the violence is a representative of Grand Ayatollah Ali As-Sistani, Sheik Mahmoud Finjan. He was As-Sistani's representative in the town of Salman Pak which is ten miles south-east of Baghdad. Sheik Finjan was shot dead

Wednesday night as he was returning from a mosque. His son and four body guards were also killed. In connection with the incident, As-Sistani's office, in the holy city of Najaf, issues a statement.

These kinds of attacks and other cases of violence are obviously a part of the insurgents' efforts to scare the Iraqis off as the elections are getting closer and closer. Most attacks at this time are targeting the majority Shiite leaders who are supporting the upcoming elections. This is their first chance to gain power since the country was formed in 1932. So far, fourteen million of Iraq's twenty six million people have registered to vote according to the White House. There are one hundred and eleven political parties. However, the results of the January 30 elections are not going to be announced until around February 15.

January 16. I have the day off.

January 17. Another contractor was injured while he was coming to the "Anaconda" air base in a U.S. military convoy. He is telling us that he saw a fourteen year old boy throw a piece of metal on him while his convoy was passing the volatile northern city of Mosul and badly hit his head. We cleaned the bloody spot on his head and put a bandage on it.

The attacks on the members of the Iraqi police, security forces and National Guard have visibly intensified as there are about two weeks left until the Iraqi elections, and several top U.S. military commanders have acknowledged that the elections are not going to be perfect, at least in some predominantly Sunni areas, such as Anbar province, Baghdad, adjacent areas and some other cities. They don't exclude the possibility that a surprise attack by the insurgents can cause a lot of casualties. That is an indication that, as the elections are approaching, the security situation is not completely under the control of the coalition forces.

In spite of the increased number of attacks, there is currently a relative calm, which might be an indication that more attacks are being prepared by the insurgents. Some soldiers like Sergeant M. say that this relative calm means the insurgents are preparing "something big" for the elections, which is "very scary." Everybody is nervous to a different extent, because everybody understands that things can get out of control at any moment prior to the elections.

The situation once again proves that the capture of Fallujah did not "break the backbone of the insurgency," as the U.S. marine commanders stated at the time. It is becoming obvious that insurgents simply left the area and scattered to other areas, mainly to the Baghdad and Mosul area.

Chapter 42

Possible Strategic Implications of the Iraq War

My impression is that the Iraq War is the last U.S. war overseas. The following incoming information points to the possibility that, by the end of the Iraq War, the United States will no longer be a superpower: the gradual and steady fall of the U.S. dollar, a huge U.S. budget deficit, and the colossal and unexpected expenses of the war. The leaders of terrorist organizations have indicated that the U.S.'s involvement in the wars in Afghanistan and Iraq was a carefully thought-out plan. In at least two separate statements, Osama Bin Laden acknowledged the existence of such a plan, to make the U.S. economy "bleed" like they made the former Soviet Union "bleed" before its demise.

It is becoming increasingly clear that it is not possible to completely defeat insurgency and terrorism. Their cells can be destroyed and financial support can be cut off. However, other similar kinds of organizations will emerge in their place unless the geopolitical reasons causing insurgency and terrorism are resolved. Fundamentally, there should be a more balanced policy aimed at the situation between Israel and its Arab neighbors. And, of course, as a part of the solution of the Israeli-Palestinian conflict, should be the creation of the two states: Israel and Palestine.

The futures of Iraq and Afghanistan should be decided by the people of these countries, with the help of the international community and international organizations, such as the U.N. Otherwise, the involvement of other countries unilaterally would always be perceived as interference, and it would further alienate these countries, thus creating a basis for insurgency. As for Iraqi insurgency, it should be made clear who and where the insurgents and terrorists are. Are they the same or are they different, with different agendas and political purposes? It is very important to define those differences.

Given all these factors, the next few decades will most likely see the U.S. lose its sole grip on world affairs, and new superpowers will emerge. One of the likely candidates is China, which has successfully managed to modify its political and economic systems to the requirements of the present time. In the new era, the most effective factors of influence are going to be economic rather than military means. A good example has been Russia, which has effectively used an economic expansionist policy towards its neighbors, the former Soviet republics, for the past several years.

Chapter 43

Another Mission Behind the Wire

January 18. We are preparing for tomorrow's mission with the Civil Affairs Unit.

It is going to be an interesting mission. We will be going to three villages to work on water purification projects. Everybody is doing his or her part. Commanders are carefully planning security and other organizational issues. Soldiers are cleaning and checking their weapons.

January 19. It is 9:00 am. We are at a briefing where security and other important information related to the mission is being discussed. We start to move out of the base at 9:30 am as scheduled. The mission includes fourteen people: commanders, soldiers who provide security in case of an attack, and three interpreters. There are two local Iraqi interpreters and myself.

We try to exit the base through the North gate but we are stopped at the gate. The guard tells us that there are IED-s (improvised explosive devices) set up by the insurgents outside of the gate so we have to leave through the East gate.

We visit three water purification projects in three separate villages: Ar-Rafaiya, Ibn Al-Khatib and Albu-Karwan.

We are greeted by Sheikh Hussein and other leaders of this region. They offer us soft drinks and cake. As soon as we arrive several children from the village surround us. They are shouting and asking for gifts. In such conditions it is becoming very difficult to provide proper security but all of us are carefully watching the villagers' hands and moves, and of course our security personnel are at full attention.

Now we are in the second village. I see a group of women with children at one of the houses. Our Humvees are not very far from the house on the road. Suddenly, one of the women from the group comes up towards me. I know it is risky but I also move towards her, understanding that she needs something. Although I want to help her I am not unaware that this is a dangerous situation. I am carefully watching the woman's hands and what is going on at the house. The woman first thinks that I do not speak Arabic and she is trying to explain something using her hands. Then, when I ask her, in Arabic, what she needs she is very happy that I understand her. She is franticly telling me that she needs lotion for her hands and toys for the children. The woman is quite young but her hands are very dry and in terrible shape, obviously because of hard work and frequent washing. She keeps talking and talking to me and her face is not covered as it is supposed to be when an Iraqi woman is talking to a man, especially in a village environment. I look around to make sure that there are no Iraqi men; otherwise this situation might cause unnecessary trouble for us. Despite these risks, I feel sorry for the woman and I tell her to wait. I rush towards our vehicle to check for lotion and toys but unfortunately none of them are left. We have already distributed everything on the way to this village. I check with one of our commanders and he says there is nothing left. I go back to the woman and explain the situation. She is very upset but thanks me anyway. I promise that when I come next time I will bring lotions and toys. I can see in her eyes that she believes me and while I am leaving she smiles and waves at me. I see that other women and children at the house are waving at me as well. Then, I get the idea to take a picture with them. I ask permission from my commander and I ask him to take my picture with them. I ask the women if they would allow me to take a picture with them and their children and they happily agreed. It is now a great picture in my album, with smiling Iraqi women and children. I feel very sorry for these pleasant people because they live in such poor conditions in a very rich country. This is very unfortunate.

In the third village I met the brother of our local translator, Salman. Our other Iraqi interpreter, Eva, is from the volatile Diyala province. She is an Iraqi Christian. Christians comprise only about five percent of Iraq's twenty six million people. Eva is an interesting person. She has to live on the base because insurgents have already tried to kill her because of her work with the U.S. troops.

The water purification projects which we are supporting financially are designed to make the water potable for the villagers. This is still one of the main problems in the country so far. People must frequently get drinking water from canals, which leads to different illnesses. This problem was neglected at the time of Saddam Hussein.

Lieutenant Colonel K., our commander had a number of meetings and discussions with representatives of the villages.

Although everything is going well so far, I feel some tension during the entire mission. Our soldiers are standing by carefully providing security while we are doing our job: talking to the Iraqis and observing the sites. At one point, one of our security people approaches me and asks me to tell a villager not to stand behind K. The villager changes his position but in a minute he comes back behind our commander again. The soldier and I strongly warn him not to stand there again and the soldier takes a position behind the commander.

Several hours have now passed and our mission is coming to an end. We are returning to the base. When we approach the North gate it is still blocked by our troops. We are told that the IED's are not cleared yet. We are waiting but it is not clear when we will be able to enter the gate. Lieutenant Colonel K. orders us to go around the field to another entrance of the base. At this point we can see how the country is becoming more dangerous and tense as the elections, which are now only ten days away, approach.

In the meantime, the U.S. intelligence community predicts that the security situation in Iraq will, most likely, not improve after the election. In fact, the situation may deteriorate, possibly to the level of civil war.

A particularly grim future for post-election Iraq was envisioned earlier this month by a retired Air Force Lieutenant General Brent Scowcroft, who was a national security adviser to the President Bush's father, President George H.W. Bush. According to Mr. Scowcroft the Iraqi elections could deepen the conflict and "We may be seeing an incipient civil war."

The assessment of the State Department's intelligence bureau is also pessimistic, as is the assessment of the main U.S. intelligence community, the CIA and the Pentagon's Defense Intelligence Agency. Those ideas were discussed at a recent U.S. intelligence community conference.

January 20. I am at the military convoy staging area. Two Turkish contractors are talking to me about an incident which took place earlier. They are saying that they were beaten by Iraqi drivers-contractors who were a part of the same U.S. military convoy. They took their driver's manifest and other documents, demanding money as a ransom. Sergeant Mata is taking all the necessary information to address the issue.

Later on the day together with the Turks, U.S. military police and KBR security we are going to identify the drivers who took the Turks' manifest.

We find one of the drivers at his truck. He fits the earlier description given by the Turks. He is a tall and strong young man, and he walks with a slight limp. I talk to him and find out that he is an Iraqi from the north. When we ask about the manifest he says that he has already returned it to the Turkish drivers' friend, named Abu Muhammed. He says that Abu Muhammed is a Turk but speaks Arabic as well.

Together with the Iraqi driver we go looking for Abu Muhammed.

In a little while, Abu Muhammed approaches us himself with the other Turks and confirms that he indeed has the manifest. We ask the owners of the manifest to look at it to make sure that this is the right one.

The Iraqi driver explains to me that the initial reason why he took the manifest was that the Turk, as a result of an accident, damaged the cabin of his truck and he wanted to make sure that the Turk would repair it. In the end, when we ask the Iraqi if he needs paperwork about the incident to make sure his truck gets repaired, he says, "No." So, the incident is resolved and everybody gets back to work.

January 21. Today marks my ninth month since I came to Iraq.

On my way to work I meet a young soldier. He says that he is going to be in Iraq for ten months because he has already spent two months in Kuwait. Before his Iraqi assignment he has been in Afghanistan for one year.

He thinks that the security situation in Iraq is much more dangerous than in Afghanistan because of the more active insurgency in Iraq.

Chapter 44

A Dangerous Mission to the Village

January 22. Today we are going on our next mission with the Civil Affairs Unit. The destination is Al-Hatamiya, which is located in the Balad area, to the north of Baghdad. The population is predominantly Shiite Muslims.

It is 9:00 am. We are still at the briefing. The commanders inform us that this mission is very dangerous for several reasons. First, a bomb is disclosed in that direction. Secondly, the village and the area are aware of the fact that we are coming, which obviously means that the insurgents also know about it. Additionally, the area is an important potential target for the insurgents because there is a police station, a polling station for the upcoming elections, and a school. The insurgents also vowed to attack the polling centers. Particularly, Abu Musaib Az-Zarqawi recently declared war on the elections on his organization's website. Police stations across the country are under intense attacks by the insurgents.

That is why we are urged to be especially careful and pay attention to what is going on around us.

At 9: 30am we are moving out of the base through the North gate. It is about a thirty-minute ride. The weather is nice and it is beautiful outside. The Iraqis are working on the fields along the road. Children are waving and greeting us, and we wave back.

We are entering the village. The narrow, ancient streets and houses make us a perfect target for the insurgents. We are visiting an unfinished building that will be a future medical clinic. It is being built by the Iraqi contractors with our funding. One of them meets us at the building. He says that Sheikh Yussef is responsible for the project. I am taking a picture on the upper floor of the building, with the village in the background. It is a wonderful view from here. Iraqis are quietly walking along the street, busy with their daily lives. I see a man praying in front of his house. Farther down the street, children are playing soccer; at another house, a woman is washing cloth.

Lieutenant Colonel K., Major C. and I are accompanied by Sergeant A., who is providing the security. Now we are going to the police station around the corner. The Chief of the police station and a dozen Iraqi police officers are waiting for us. Colonel K. and Major C. are discussing the upcoming elections. I am providing translation during the entire meeting. Sergeant A. and several Iraqi police members are outside of the office. Soldiers are positioned around the building, ready to deter an attack at any minute.

Colonel K. is asking about the preparations for the upcoming elections. The Chief says that everything is going well; the morale and readiness of the police station is high and the villagers are ready to vote.

Colonel K. mentions that a bomb was found in the village. The Chief replies that the bomb was found by someone from another village and brought to them to help to defuse it. So, the bomb was set up in another village. And, it was subsequently defused without any casualties.

K. asks if there has been discussion about providing the police station with heavy automatic weapons, particularly before the upcoming elections, in order to strengthen the security. The Chief simply says, "No."

We are completing our meeting and are ready to leave. A police station employee approaches us and asks about his garden and grape yard, which he can no longer explore. He says that the land is located on the "Anaconda" air base. The last time that he tried to approach it, he was stopped by U.S. soldiers who made a warning shot in the air.

Lieutenant Colonel K. and the other Lieutenant Colonel who is teaming with us tell him to come to the base to meet with them in order to help solve the problem.

In the next minute, we are getting an order that it is time to leave. Everybody is rushing to the designated Humvees and beginning to head towards the base.

On the way to the base, I notice that pictures and posters of Ayatollah Ali As-Sistani are posted everywhere, showing him as a candidate for the coalition of Shiite parties. I mention to Lieutenant Colonel and Major C. that, because of the existing tension between Shiites and Sunnis, it would be more appropriate to have several candidates from both main communities. Colonel K. says that it is a reflection of reality, because a majority of the population in this particular village is Shiite Muslim. Yet, I saw the same situation with the posters in other villages that were made up of a mix of Sunni and Shiite residents.

We are approaching the base. Fortunately, the mission went well and without incident. We are safely returning to the base. It is a success each time that we return from a mission without casualties. Unfortunately, it is not the case all the time in every unit. War is war.

Chapter 45

Getting Closer to the Elections

January 23. Today is my day off. I talked to my wife and my daughter over the phone. They are still very worried about me. My daughter tells me what is going on in school and that she is getting good grades. I am happy for her. She is a good kid but I feel that it is very important to be with her at this time. But, unfortunately I am still far from home.

January 24. I am at the military convoy staging area. There several of soldiers waiting to leave with the convoys. We are making last minute preparations. Most of the military convoys today are going south, towards the border with Kuwait.

Also today, a car bomb exploded outside the At-Taf mosque in southwestern Baghdad, where Shiites are celebrating one of Islam's most important holidays, Eid Al-Adha, or Feast of Sacrifice. The Feast coincides with the yearly pilgrimage to Mecca in Saudi Arabia.

The most notorious rebel, Abu Musaib Az-Zarqawi, in his latest web audio messages accused the Iraqi Shiites of siding with the U.S. troops, particularly during the assault on Fallujah. Shiites make up an estimated sixty percent of the Iraq's twenty six million people.

According to U.S. and Iraqi officials, most of the country is secure enough for the upcoming elections, but Baghdad and three predominantly Sunni Arab provinces: Anbar, Ninevah and Salahaddin, are still an issue.

Our local translator, Salman Safi, says that the security situation is, unfortunately, not good. As an example, he refers to the volatile city of Ramadi, where the entire police station resigns and nobody is controlling the situation there except the U.S. troops. Salman is very upset and worried. He says that the current security situation gives him a "heart pain."

January 25. I am at the military convoy staging area. Several U.S. convoys are ready to leave. We are told that, beginning January 27, there will be no missions outside of the base, including for my Civil Affairs Unit which is regularly going to the villages for different civil projects. This new order is connected with the security measures which are being taken before the upcoming elections in the country. The elections are only five days away from now.

January 26. I am at the military convoy staging area. Several contractors, Egyptian and Turkish truck drivers, are asking us to help unload their cargo. They are carrying a variety of cargo for the U.S. and coalition forces. As a new security measure, the U.S. military police took their cellular phones as soon as they entered the base. As the elections approach, the insurgency is becoming even more active and they can infiltrate U.S. military bases as they have in the past. Cellular phones are easily can be used to direct attacks.

It is about 12:00 pm. I am in the dining facility, getting ready to have my lunch when I hear several loud blasts outside. We think that it is a rocket or mortar attack and everybody rushes to the bunkers to take a cover. In several minutes, though, it becomes clear that these are controlled blasts from our troops and everybody goes back to the dining facility.

Today we were scheduled to fly by helicopter to Duvaniya, which is located in the south of the country, close to the holy Shiite city of Karbala. The mission is related to the upcoming elections but it is cancelled because of the security reasons. As the elections are getting closer the country is becoming very dangerous and unpredictable.

January 27. Today there are more casualties among our troops. Thirty one U.S. marines and soldiers are killed in a helicopter crush in the Western part of Iraq. The only possible reason sited so far is bad weather. Additionally, several U.S. soldiers died in different situations across the country. The U.S. death toll in one single day- thirty nine

U.S. service members has become the bloodiest since March 2003.

At the military convoy staging area, several contractors are asking again about their cellular phones. Their phones were taken away on January 25th by the military police during the security check. Due to the new regulations, cell phones are not allowed to be taken in to the base; otherwise they will be taken and destroyed.

Specialist K., a member of our military unit says that everybody was notified about the new regulation.

January 28. On my way to work, I heard the news that the U.S. Senator Ted Kennedy said that, "We have reached the point, when the U.S. troops being in Iraq is not productive anymore and they should be brought home." According to the news other Senators have signed the request as well.

Some soldiers are saying that this is wrong and we should be involved because the U.S. has bases in Japan, Korea, Germany and other countries, but except Kuwait we don't have any significant military presence anywhere in the Middle East in spite of the huge Middle Eastern population in the U.S. Other soldiers think that we should not have come to Iraq in the first place.

January 29. There is just one day left before the elections. Security is tightened everywhere. I come to the dining facility in the morning to have breakfast. Security guards at the facility tell us that because of security reasons, they don't want big concentrations of the people. Everybody should take food to go, rather than stay inside the facility.

The movement of military convoys in all directions is halted because of the elections and all missions for my Civil Affairs Unit, and other units I am working with, are canceled for the period prior to the elections.

Chapter 46

Historical Day and Aftermath

January 30. Today are the national elections in Iraq. The polling stations have been open since about 7 am. Security is tight everywhere; no vehicles are on the roads, borders are closed, and a curfew is imposed.

Despite the extraordinary security measures, there are nine suicide bombings, as well as mortar and rocket attacks across the country today. There are many dead and wounded Iraqis at the polling stations. We even hear reports that insurgents are identifying the Iraqis who have voted by the ink on their fingers, and immediately kill them. The U.S. embassy also comes under rocket attack in Baghdad, in the fortified Green Zone. At least one U.S. service member and a civilian have been killed, and several others are wounded.

Despite the escalated violence, the turnout of voters exceeded all the expectations. The active participation in the elections is particularly noted in the north, Kurdish areas, and the south of the country.

Joyful and tearful Iraqis are casting their ballots and hoping that this historical day will ultimately bring them a better future. Entire families—fathers and mothers with their children—are coming to the polling stations. I remember an image of a family, father and mother holding their little child's hands, coming to vote, probably for the future of their child. In the north, an elderly woman was brought to the polling station in a wheelchair.

In a contrast to all these encouraging incidents, the polling stations in the central Sunni areas remained mainly deserted and empty, in such places as: Mosul, Samarra, Baquba, Tikrit, and Fallujah.

The final official results are going to be known later. The Iraqis are electing 275 members to the Assembly, which is supposed to write a new constitution for the country and chose the President of Iraq.

President George Bush announced that the elections were a success. He says that by participating in the elections, Iraqis showed that they are "against thugs and assassins."

January 31. The elections are over and things are getting back to normal. So far, nothing extraordinary has happened, except the occasional violence. The official results are going to be announced soon. But nobody expects that with the elections all the problems in Iraq will disappear.

One of the biggest issues may be the lack of Sunni representation in the future Assembly, which will most likely add fuel to the ongoing Sunni insurgency.

In fact, Abu Musaib Az-Zarqawi has said, "We need to be ready for a long fight against the Americans."

In the midst of the violence, the plane Hercules C-130, carrying British personnel, was shot down, killing ten British soldiers. The incident happens en route from Baghdad to the "Anaconda" air base. Abu Musaib Az-Zarqawi's group claims responsibility for shooting down the plane. This was the heaviest British loss in a single day since March 2003, when the invasion started. So far, the British military has lost seventy service members.

February 1. Today I am at the military convoy staging area. Everything is quiet. The election results have not been announced yet. They are expected to be announced in about ten days, after a careful counting of the voting ballots.

February 2. While I am working at the military convoy staging area there are several control blasts, fired by our soldiers. We also had mortar and rocket attacks between 9 am and 10 am. It took about thirty minutes until the all-clear siren was sounded. I don't know if there are any casualties, but I do know that the trailer that I was sitting in was shaking during the explosions.

February 3. According to the *Associated Press*, at least 1,434 members of the U.S. military have died since the beginning of the Iraq war in March 2003.

The results of the elections have not been announced yet. In its first statement since the balloting, the Association of Muslim Scholars says that the vote lacks legitimacy because of low Sunni participation. The Association was boycotting the elections. The Association said that the election "lacks legitimacy because large portions of the people have boycotted it." As a result, they claim that the new Iraqi leadership lacks the mandate to draft a new constitution and should only be considered a temporary administration. Moreover, the statement asserts, "We make it clear to the United Nations and the International community that they should not get involved in granting this election legitimacy because such a move will open the gates of evil." However, the Association is going to respect the choice of those who voted, and if all the parties participating in the political process agree on it, they would consider the new government as a transitional one with limited powers.

Following Sunday's elections, attacks by insurgents dropped sharply, but it is still too early to assess whether that trend will continue. A similar kind of decrease in insurgent activities was noted right after the handover of power to the Interim Iraqi government in June. But shortly after, insurgents resumed their attacks.

February 4. An assumption that the decline in insurgency right after the elections was a temporary situation looks to be proving itself.

At least 26 Iraqis and two U.S. marines are killed, following a post-election lull. In the deadliest incident, insurgents stopped a minibus in the northern town of Kirkuk, ordered the Iraqi Army recruits off the bus and shot twelve of them dead, execution style. They let two Iraqi soldiers go, and ordered them to warn others against joining Iraq's U.S.-backed security and police forces. Interestingly, that particular insurgent group is one of the oldest Islamic organizations. They are called Takfir wa Al-Hijra, and they were established in 1960s in Egypt. They have been active in the Middle East for many years. This is the first time that the organization is emerging in Iraq since the invasion. They reject society, thinking it to be corrupt, and wants to establish an Islamic community based on utopian principals.

In addition to this incident, at least two U.S. marines are killed in clashes with insurgents in the volatile Anbar province, which includes Sunni triangle towns Ramadi, Fallujah, and Al-Qaim.

Chapter 47

Back to Missions and Day to Day Work

February 5. Our briefing for today's mission begins at 9:00 AM. In about 30 minutes we will move out of the base. Everybody is making final preparations: checking weapons, studying the map of the area we are going to, getting security instructions, etc. We are visiting three villages today: Jumhuriya #2 for the grand opening of the project, Al-Betera to test the water purification project there and Jumhuria #1 for the grand opening of the project. All three are water purification projects which our unit is sponsoring.

We receive a very warm reception in all three villages. We are now going to the Jumhuriya #2 village. In our humvee is Lieutenant Colonel K., Major C., Specialist G. as a gunner, and myself for the language and cultural support. On the way to the village, Captain G. approaches our vehicle and reports to Colonel K. that he received a confidential message that there are insurgents in the village. We are urged to be on alert while we approach the village.

When we arrive a representative of the village comes up to us and asks for Colonel K. and Major C. He wants to pass an official letter to them in connection with the project. I interpret for Colonel K., explaining to the villager in Arabic that, in accordance with the country's sovereignty and new rules, all issues should be directed through the City Council. K. also says that there is an American representative there who can be helpful as well. The villager, however, says that the City Council is a problem because there are a lot of people working there who have been there since Saddam Hussein's regime and that the Council is very corrupted.

While the Iraqi is talking to us and I am helping with interpretation he asks me several times if I am an Egyptian. I reply that I am an

American but of Azerbaijani origin. He doesn't believe me, however, and he keeps asking the same question over and over. Then he asks me to step aside and tells me about his background, how he joined and worked for the Iraqi National Guard. I understand that he is trying to gain my trust for some reason, probably thinking that I am not telling him truth about my country of origin. I ask him why he doesn't believe that I am an Azerbaijani, and he replies that a foreigner cannot be so fluent in Arabic. Then he again asks me to help him to communicate with Colonel K. On the way back to the base I tell Colonel K. and Major C. about this conversation with the Iraqi. They laugh.

The mission is coming to an end without any incidents and we make our way back to the base. Salman, our local interpreter is with us now in our Humvee. We picked him up on the way to the first village. I also met his brother, again. He is always helpful to us. The entire mission was a little bit tense because of the intelligence information we received. We expected an attack at any time. My impression is that insurgents are usually reluctant to attack when we are helping Iraqis. One of the reasons might be that it can create bad publicity for them, in the eyes of the local Iraqis.

February 6. Today we receive the initial results of the elections. They indicate that the United Iraqi Alliance, which has the endorsement of Iraq's top Shiite clerics, won more than two-thirds of the 3.3 million votes counted so far. This is according to the election commission. Interim Prime-Minister Ayad Allawi's list is running second with more than 579,700 votes.

The United Iraqi Alliance leaders, Ali As-Sistani, Abdul-Aziz Al-Hakim and others spent years of exile in neighboring Iran because of the suppression of Iraq's majority Shiites by Saddam Hussein regime. They are believed to have close ties with the Iranian Shiite clerics, but the top Iraqi Shiite clerics have publicly announced that they are not seeking to impose Islamic law and Islamic regime in Iraq.

In the meantime, amid increasing violence after the elections, insurgents abducted a journalist of the Italian newspaper "Manifesto" Giuliana Sgrena in Baghdad. On its internet website the Islamic group demanded the withdrawal of all Italian troops from Iraq, otherwise they threatened to kill the Italian journalist.

Also insurgents abducted several Egyptian telecommunication technicians.

As the violence continues to escalate the U.S. military reported the death of several U.S. marines and soldiers over the past few days, particularly in the volatile Babil and Anbar provinces. Several soldiers died as a result of Thursday's attack on a Stryker combat vehicle, which rolled over several anti-tank mines. Another U.S. soldier dies and seven soldiers are wounded Friday, when a roadside bomb hit their patrol near Beiji, 155 miles north of Baghdad. These casualties are reported by the U.S. military.

According to the Defense Department and Associated Press count, as of Thursday, 1,441 members of the U.S. military have died since the beginning of the Iraq war in March 2003.

At least 1,103 died as a result of hostile action. The figures include four military civilians.

February 7. I do not feel well. I must have got some sort of cold while on the previous mission on February 5.

We get several visitors on the military convoy staging area today. One Turkish contractor-driver lost his truck two months ago as a result of an insurgent attack while on his way from the Kurdish populated area called Zakhu to the U.S. "Anaconda" air base. The incident occurred near the city of Samarra where his convoy was subjected to a massive insurgent attack.

He says that the KBR company has been looking for his truck since then.

He asks us to facilitate a meeting between KBR and representatives of his company. He says that he now knows the exact location of his truck and cargo, but he acknowledges that they are completely burnt.

His final purpose in recovering the truck is to get compensation from his company.

February 8. Concerns began to grow about the possibility of a Shiite Islamic rule in Iraq, following the example of the neighboring Iran, when an early tally of voters showed a strong lead for Iraqi Shiite parties supported by the top influential Shiite clerics, like grand Ayatolla Ali As-Sistani. But the U.S. administration officials, including Vice-President Dick Cheney and Defense Secretary Donald Rumsfeld, brushed away those concerns saying that they don't believe that this would happen because there are enough reasonable people among the Iraqis to balance out any religious extremists. They also indicated, however, that in the end these were the Iraqi elections, meaning that it is up to the Iraqis to decide their future and that everything is supposed to be done in accordance with their culture and customs. At the same time, Mr. Rumsfeld cited that if those concerns prove to be true, then it would be a "terrible mistake."

In my opinion, this is a very real possibility which is not publicized much by the Iraqi Shiite leaders, at least not at the present stage. The majority of the current Shiite leaders have been in exile in Iran for a long time and they, undoubtedly, have developed close ties with the Iranian theological and clerical circles including those who are in the Iranian leadership. There are already indications that elements of the Islamic law are going to be included in the upcoming constitution which is supposed to be written by the 275 member Assembly, which in turn, is supposed to have been elected as a result of the past Iraqi elections.

Cheney also added that, "In the final analysis, the bottom line for everybody to remember that, this is not going to be an Iraqi version of America."

February 9. I have a terrible flue and I stay in my place but I am still helping the Civil Affairs Unit communicate with some Turkish contractors working in our building. Unfortunately, this is no time to be sick. There is too much work to do.

February 10. On my way to work one of the Turkish contractors, Suad, approaches me and starts telling me about an incident which took place yesterday. He says he went to the AT&T calling center to make a call using his calling card. One of the U.S. soldiers, who was next to him, asked him to look at his calling card for a second. Eventually, that soldier kept calling, using Suad's calling card, because he later found out that a lot of his minutes were used. According to Suad, when he was trying to say something to object, the soldier made a hand gesture and said, "Go, go away." Suad described the soldier as an African American and he gave other detailed descriptions. While talking to me, Suad looks very upset. I am telling him that I will talk to my Unit about the incident.

February 11. I talk to Major C., deputy commander of the Civil Affairs Unit, about the incident with the Turkish contractor. He says that similar incidents have already happened before and he asks me to get more detailed information, particularly about the time of the incident and the appearance of the soldier. Major C. tells me that the military police suspects one soldier who continues to do the same with different foreign contractors on the base.

Later on, I talk to Suad again. He says that the soldier is about 175 cm. tall, skinny, and African- American. Suad also says that he was dressed in Army sports shirt with "Army" sign on it and black sports pants. That's why Suad couldn't see his name. In regular Army uniforms the last names of the soldiers are visible. But Suad was sure that if he sees the soldier again he could identify him. I go to report the collected information back to Major C.

February 12. Major C. finds out that there were other incidents with the same soldier, Specialist A., who was in our Unit before. C. finds out that calls were made from Suad's calling card to the State of Louisiana which is the native state of A.. In addition to this information, when we showed Suad A.'s picture he recognized him. According to Major C. and Specialist K., since all these allegations have been proved, Specialist A. might expect a dishonorable discharge and subsequent expulsion from the Army and even the possibility of being jailed. Major C. says he will pass all the information to the relevant people. In the meantime he gave another calling card to Suad to use as compensation.

Chapter 48

Ashura: Concern for Sectarian Violence and the Political Process

Thursday is the first day of the Islamic month of Muharram, or Ashura, which is the holiest day of the Shiite Muslim calendar, marking the death of Imam Hussein, the grandson of the prophet Muhammed. Imam Hussein was killed in a 7th-century struggle for a power of Halif (head of the Islamic state) and leadership in the Islamic world. There were many casualties last March, when simultaneous explosions ripped through crowds of worshippers at Shiite Muslim shrines in Baghdad, Karbala, and Najaf. During Ashura, thousands of Shiites from around the world gather at Hussein's tomb in Karbala and other Shiite holy sites in Iraq.

On the eve of this major Shiite religious holiday, Iraqi officials announce that they would close the country's borders for five days this month to prevent any possible violence. Lately, insurgents are increasingly targeting the Shiites, apparently trying to ignite a civil war between the Sunnis and Shiites. The Sunnis are the core of the Iraqi insurgency.

In the meantime, Iraqi officials announce that the results of the elections are going to be delayed for several more days. However, due to preliminary results, there is already some speculation that the United Iraqi Alliance, the Kurdish List, and Allawi's ticket are leading. Therefore, the United Shiite Alliance of Iraqi parties will be seeking the Prime-Ministerial position, the Kurdish List will be looking for the mostly ceremonial Presidency, and the third top post will likely be given to either the current Interim Prime Minister Allawi or the current President Yawer.

February 13. My day off. We are having mortar and rocket attacks during the day. Contractors are among the killed and wounded. Each such incident is a tragedy that affects many families. This is very unfortunate, but we know that this is a reality of the war.

February 14. Further preliminary results show that the Shiite-dominated United Iraqi Alliance can win about 140 seats in the future Assembly. The Coalition of Kurdish Parties has won about 70 seats, and the remaining 30-35 seats can be taken by the Iraqi List of the current Interim Prime Minister Ayad Allawi. Accordingly, Ayatollah Ali As-Sistani's supported representatives of the Iraqi Alliance are looking for the influential and key position of Prime Minister in the future government, while the candidate from the Kurdish Parties, Jalal Talabani, is seeking the mostly ceremonial position of the President. Most likely the Speaker of the Assembly position will be given to Ayad Allawi, the current Interim Prime Minister or the current President Sunni Muslim Al-Yawer. Of course, this all might change by the time the official results are announced.

February 15. We are solving some technical and administrative issues related to the repair of our building. Later, I am at the military convoy staging area, where several foreign contractors are trying to get identification badges for their trucks. This is a very sensitive security issue, and we are trying to carefully verify each person's identity and information. My role here is important; I am trying to verify their personal information in Arabic and Turkish and convey it to the relevant U.S. service members. Typically, these contractors do not speak English at all. One of the contractors is acting very suspiciously; he doesn't "remember" much of his personal information. So, I am trying to pay more attention to his case, and I report to my commanders that there might be a problem with this person. The appropriate security personnel are informed about the case.

Chapter 49

On Missions Again Outside of the Base

February 16. Today we are going on our next mission. We are planning to visit three villages: An-Nazaha, Jamil Umron and Ali Hameed. All three water purification projects are funded and supported by the U.S. Army. The purpose of the visit to Jamil Umron and Ali Hameed to oversee the progress of the project and the aim of the visit to An-Nazaha is to discuss further details of the next steps of the project there.

Lieutenant Colonel K., Major C., Captain G., Sergeant R., Specialist K., Specialist J., local interpreter Salman Safee and I are participating in the mission. Additionally, several soldiers from other units are joining us to provide security during the mission.

The weather is nice and we are all in a good mood as we move out of the base, towards the villages. We reach the villages in about thirty minutes. They are close to each other. I like the environment here, it is greener and there are more people outside greeting us. I take a few pictures around the villages. In one of the villages Captain G. and I approach a school which is half built by local Iraqis. We ask them who is funding the school. A local Iraqi replies that the school being financially supported by an American non-profit company called "Washington," located in Tikrit. We are glad that more and more companies are getting involved and investing in the reconstruction of Iraq.

The mission comes to an end and we make our way back to the base.

Later in the evening we are going to the dining facility on the base to have dinner with Salman, our local translator. We then decide to go to the internet café. Then, we return to our place where we stay. On the way to our place Salman shows me the Moon and three colored circles that surround it. He tells me that according to the Iraqi legend, it means that very soon it is going to rain, as he says, "Invitation to rain." Salman tells me about it quietly, almost whispering, and it gives his words a special mystical sound.

Chapter 50

Difficult Political Process and Continuing Violence

In the meantime, according to the United Iraqi Alliance, two main candidates are emerging for the post of Prime Minister. First, there is Ahmad Chalabi, a former Pentagon favorite who fell out of favor last year after claims that he passed intelligence information to Iran. Chalabi, 58, represents the Iraqi National Congress. The second candidate is Al-Jaafari, who lived in London at the time of Saddam Hussein's reign. He is the leader of the Dawa Party. According to the Alliance, Al-Jaafari is most likely the final candidate from the alliance, which is reportedly going to take 140 out of the 275 seats in the National Assembly. Al-Jaafari is a moderate Shiite politician who fled a brutal crackdown by Saddam Hussein in 1980. He is also 58 years-old and a physician by profession.

He suggests drafting a constitution that will be based not only on Islam. According to him, "Islam should be the official religion of the country, one of the main sources for legislation, along with other sources that do not harm Muslim sensibilities."

Al-Jaafari considers the security situation to be his priority if he is elected Prime-Minister. He also says that he is not going to push for the U.S. and coalition forces to withdraw their troops from Iraq anytime soon.

So, the results of the elections are as follows: The United Iraqi Alliance received 48%, the Kurdish Alliance earned 26%, and Allawi's List won 14%. Thus, 140 seats are going to be taken by the UIA, and the Kurdish Alliance and Allawi's List will receive the rest accordingly. The 275-member Assembly is supposed to draft the Constitution and chose the Presidential Council, which will consist of the President and two Vice-Presidents. They will also elect the Prime Minister of Iraq.

In the evening, before Salman leaves, he tells me that another of his friends, an Iraqi National Guardsman, has recently been killed by the insurgents. Each time that a friend is killed, it seems to him that he is going to be next. I ask Salman to be careful when he is outside of the base.

According to Salman, the information about the Iraqis who cooperate with the coalition forces is being passed by the soldiers of the New Iraqi Army to the insurgents. Salman says that they are mainly bad people—former thieves and other kinds of criminals. Also, Salman says that these Iraqi soldiers search the local Iraqis when they come to the U.S. base for work, so they know who has money, and they pass their names to different criminal groups for abduction or for ransom. As an example, Salman reminds me of the kidnapping of another one of our local translators, Firas, who had to pay a ransom to be released.

Salman says that kidnappers knew that Firas had money, because they were usually the ones who searched him when he came to the base to work. Before the kidnappers released Firas, they tied him to a bed and beat him badly.

February 18. The negotiations are still continuing among the Shiite coalition in connection with the key post of the future Prime Minister. It will obviously take some time. According to the observers, until the Prime Minister candidate is determined, the status of the President and two Vice Presidents will be on hold. The selection of Prime Minister doesn't have any specific deadline.

In the meantime, the violence in different parts of Iraq is continuing.

Several explosions in Baghdad kill and wound a number of Iraqis. The U.S. military announces that two U.S. service members died in a vehicle accident on Wednesday in Iraq's Babil province. Another soldier died of a non-combat injury on the same day, at a base near Tikrit. Two soldiers also died in separate vehicle accidents in Diyala and Balad. On Tuesday, a service member was killed during security operations conducted in Iraq's volatile Anbar province. According to the *Associated Press,* 1,470 U.S. military members have died in Iraq since the beginning of the war.

February 19. Today's morning mission outside of the base is cancelled again due to security reasons. This happens from time to time when we receive relevant intelligence information about security threats.

Instead, we spend the morning visiting the Iraqi National Guard's dining facility. Captain G., Sergeant R., a representative from the Public Affairs Unit, and I are here to prepare material about the Iraqi guardsmen.

The representative from the Public Affairs Unit is conducting an interview with two Iraqi guardsmen, Muhammed and Bashar, and I am helping with the interpreting.

The Iraqi National Guard is being trained by the coalition forces. On Monday, we are planning another visit to the dining facility to take interviews with Iraqi guardsmen. After this, we plan to go to the military convoy staging area to take interviews with foreign national contractors working for the U.S. Army.

February 20. Today is my day off. And today is also exactly eleven months since I left home and headed to Fort Benning, Georgia, where I soon left for Iraq.

February 21. We are going on our next mission outside of the base. We are planning to visit three villages: Fadus, Ash-Shahabi, and Al-Betera. There is a grand opening of one of the water filtration sites. We are driving in several Humvees, when suddenly, our Humvee turns over. Our gunner, Specialist J., falls on me, but there are no serious injuries. The road is really bad and requires much effort from our drivers.

We are approaching one of the schools in the village that we support.

The director and staff of the school come out and meet us at the entrance. I help to translate between everyone. Generally, the school looks to be in a good shape.

We ask the director of the school if he needs anything specifically for the teachers or the school. But, interestingly, he cannot clearly identify the needs for teachers and school.

We continue on to other villages. During the drive, Major C. says that he has a bad feeling about that day's mission. But fortunately, we complete the mission successfully and return to the base without any incidents.

Although we had planned on taking more interviews with the Iraqi National Guardsmen, they had already left the dining facility by the time we arrived. The Public Affairs Unit is very interested in preparing material about the emerging Iraqi security forces and Army.

Now we are driving to the military convoy staging area. We meet several Turkish and Arabic contractors-truck drivers who are riding with the U.S. military as part of the military convoys. Their job is very dangerous and insurgents frequently target them; the number of casualties among them is quite high. We ask many questions and learn about the contractors' needs, many of which are not being met.

After we finish this mission, the representative from the Public Affairs Unit thanks me for my help and tells me that their office would like to prepare an article about me for the military newspaper *Anaconda Times*. He says that the newspaper is being distributed on the U.S. military bases and twenty copies of each issue are being sent to the Pentagon as well. We agreed to meet on Friday at 1:00 pm.

Today also marked 10 months since the day I arrived in Iraq.

February 22. Today's mission is cancelled for security reasons. Instead, I spend all day at the military convoy staging area, helping to solve different issues related to the foreign national contractors working with the U.S. Army. Right now, I have a visitor, who is an Iraqi Kurd from the north of the country. His truck broke down near the city of Samarra and he needs help picking it up.

Chapter 51

Trying to get Closer to the Iraqis to Win their Trust

February 23. We are going on our next mission in the morning. As usual, our briefing is at 9:00 am. This time the mission includes only Lieutenant Colonel K., Major C., translator Salman and I from our Civil Affairs Unit. Several soldiers from other units are added to our mission to provide security. At 9:30 AM we move out. In about one hour we reach 14 Ramadan village. This village is comprised of mainly Sunni Muslims.

The purpose of our visit to observe the water purification project and determine what else is needed for its implementation.

Our translator Salman says that, in his opinion, the project should cost only $30-35,000, but instead $120,000 has been spent so far.

14 Ramadan village is located in the Dijeil district of the Balad region of the Salahaddin province. The village is about 40km from LSA "Anaconda" U.S. air base. This is one of the most remote villages we have visited so far.

As we leave the village, the local kids try to run next to our Humvees. I am telling them to be careful but they are still running and suggesting we buy watches, souvenirs and other stuff. I noticed a cute little girl running next to my Humvee. I give her some money and she is very happy and smiling. She reminded me of my own daughter.

We approach the second village, which is called Ibrahim Ad-Dalash which has a majority Shiite population. Here also the purpose is to visit the water purification sites which we are sponsoring. The project is going well although, as usual, there are some problems mainly related to corruption and to competition between different tribes for more money. As a result, the projects are frequently being hindered.

We are moving to the next village, Albu-Feizi, the final destination in today's mission. This is a site visit of the school and the water project. The population is mainly Shiites and we can clearly tell by their clothing, different flags on the top of the houses and even appearance. After being in Iraq for a while I have learnt to distinguish Shiites and Sunnis even by appearance. For example, the Shiites tend to have slightly darker skin.

We return to the base. Thanks to God, we again have no casualties.

February 24. We are going on a mission again. After our usual briefing we are moving out of the base. We visit two villages: Hatamia and Albu Hassan. In Hatamia we make a site visit of the water purification project facility and the medical clinic. We had visited the medical clinic before, but since then nothing was done, the status of the construction is the same.

We meet the Chief of the police in the Hatamia village. Lieutenant Colonel K. talks to him about the criminal situation, activities of the insurgents in the area and other issues.

K. says, as a supervisor at a police department in North Carolina, he is interested in talking about these issues and in exchanging opinions and sharing experiences. The Iraqi policeman says that they have just one law in Iraq which covers all possible criminal situations and usually, they deal with everyday casual situations.

K. says that in the U.S., they have different laws for different criminal cases. K. also asks the Iraqi if there is some kind of regional emergency calling center to deal with family conflicts and other social problems. The Iraqi police Chief replies that they don't have such services similar to the ones in the U.S.

Then we visit Albu Hassan village also for the water purification project.

This is a very nice hilly village with many trees and grass but you also smell sewage as soon as you enter the village. On our way to the village we found a rocket on the road. Obviously insurgents buried it, expecting us. We see it in time and it is immediately defused.

When we enter Albu-Hassan village I see a big house on the hill with a nice woody yard surrounded by a fence. It is next to the water project which we support.

I am told that this is the local leader, Sheikh Wadi's residence and guest house.

Hatamia and Albu-Hassan are both predominantly Shiite and there are still many election posters which have not been taken down yet after the elections. In many posters I see a picture of top Shiite leader, Grand Ayatollah Ali As-Sistani.

I like Albu-Hassan village, with its narrow streets and medieval style houses made of mud. But I notice that the looks the villagers are giving us are not friendly. When we pass, the villagers greet us but their eyes are not smiling. Even the children angrily follow us with their looks. Women rashly cover their faces and turn away from us. These villagers give me a very unpleasant feeling. Obviously the villagers are not happy with our presence in the village, and if there are insurgents in the village, it is a perfect place to attack us because of the narrow streets and the complicated layout of the houses. I relay my observation to Lieutenant Colonel K., and he agrees with me. He says that this particular village is really not very friendly towards the Americans, even though we are trying to help them with a water purification project.

We finish our mission and return safely to the base. At the North gate we are told that an unexploded rocket was found right after we left the base and it has been successfully defused by our troops.

Chapter 52

Publicity of the War Experience

Upon returning to the base, I see that the representatives of the Public Affairs Unit are waiting for me at the building where I live. They are getting ready to take a video interview with me. According to them, the material is going to be used for newsreel on the bases, military newspapers, and possibly as a piece that will be sold to major U.S. news agencies. They tell me that their commanders want them to prepare material about me because of my foreign language proficiency, educational background, and work experience. They also plan on taping me on Saturday, while I am working on my mission outside of the base.

February 25. Our planned mission to Talil U.S. military base is cancelled because of a lack of aircrafts. But, it is planned for a later date and Lieutenant Colonel K., Major C., and I are going to participate in it.

Talil is located in the south of the country, closer to the Shiite holy cities of Najaf and Karbala, ancient historic ruins, and sites of the country called "Rur." It is going to be a very interesting and dangerous trip.

February 26. We are going on our next mission. This time, we are visiting two villages: Al-Adala and Garagul. Garagul means "black flower" in Turkic languages. Out of curiosity, I ask around if there are any ancestral roots or connections with the Turkic ethnos in this village, since the name of the village is obviously Turkic. But nobody knows, and the current population consists of Arabs.

In both villages, there are grand openings of the water purification projects, which are each about 95% complete. The Sheikhs and residents of the area are meeting us. As was planned, our Public Affairs

Unit representatives are with us, recording and taking my picture while I am interpreting for our commanders, talking to the Sheikhs, residents, and local Iraqi children.

In the Al-Adala village, when Salman introduces me to the Sheikh and the residents, he tells them that I am an Egyptian. Although I tell them that I am an American of Azerbaijani origin who speaks Arabic, they still do not seem to believe it. Our mission in the village is accomplished and now we are leaving. I jokingly tell the villagers that I will pass their greetings on to the people in my neighborhood in Egypt. It sounds funny in Arabic, and the Iraqis are laughing. I think they realize that I am joking, because they are smiling and greeting me. I am glad that I have made a good connection with them.

On the way to Garagul, there is a little incident. We notice that a boy is standing on the road and holding wires in his hands. We take all necessary precautions and stop our Humvees. Captain G. asks me to go with him to find out information about the boy's situation. We carefully approach the boy, at the same time looking around. It might be an ambush by the insurgents. The boy tells us that he brought the wires with him from home because he needs to tie hashish together after he cuts it on the field.

I interpret for Captain G., who tells the boy that he is taking the wires from him and would return them to him later. At that moment, I am looking around and thinking that if it is an ambush and insurgents start shooting, the boy might be caught in the crossfire. In the back of my mind, I decide that if that happens, I would grab the boy and push him on the ground to protect him from the bullets. Fortunately, nothing happens.

We are finishing our mission and now moving towards the base.

The Public Affairs Unit representatives are telling me that they are satisfied with the recordings and pictures that they have taken. They are sure that it is going to be a good material for TV programming and publication.

We are entering the base from the North gate and approaching the mosque area, where our place is located. The representatives of the Public Affairs Unit record a final interview with me. Later, the articles and video newsreels get picked up by other newspapers and websites back in the U.S. It is a good publicity about our work in Iraq.

February 27. I am trying to organize a soccer team. We play soccer from time to time after work and more people are joining us. We usually play with Turkish contractors. But, the field is so dusty and it might be quite dangerous to play on the open field.

Today, while we are playing at about 6 pm, there are mortar and rocket attacks on the base. The alarm siren goes off, but we decide to continue to play. Soon, the military police approach us and tell us to take a cover. We have to stop the game and everybody leaves. When my wife learns that I am playing soccer in Iraq, she gets very concerned. She writes me in a message, "How you can play soccer in a war zone? Isn't it dangerous? A bomb can fall on your head." I jokingly reply that she shouldn't worry, because if the bomb falls on my head it would get broken on it and it would be a waste of money for the insurgents. When we talk on the phone later, she tells me that I am never serious and war is not a joke.

February 28. We are having a mission today in two villages: An-Nazaha and Al-Fadouz. We are going to visit our project sites to check their status and find out what else is needed to complete them. But at the last minute, the mission is cancelled because we get intelligence information that there might be an insurgent ambush.

On my way to the military convoy staging area, I meet another U.S. linguist named Leila. We were in the same group at Fort Benning, and we arrived on the same day in Iraq.

I remember that while at Fort Benning, she was very concerned about whether she was going to survive in Iraq. I told her that she was going to be alright.

We are glad to see each other and she tells me that she is going to leave for the U.S. for a vacation before coming back for a second year of service. She also intends to ask to be transferred to the Special

Forces Unit after she comes back. I tell her that it might be dangerous for her. But, she replies that because she has faith in God, she is not scared. I see how she has changed, becoming more experienced and less fearful. I wish Leila all the best. We hope to see each other again.

I am also thinking of staying for a second year; I will probably decide by the end of May. Either way, by that time I am planning to go for a vacation to the U.S. and decide if I am officially completing my deployment in Iraq.

March 1. Today I am at the military convoy staging area. We are getting information that there are demonstrations going on in the Shiite-dominated Sadr city protesting a new rule to make Saturday a day off. Demonstrators are chanting that they reject it because it is a "Jewish holiday."

The influential Sunni Association of Muslim Scholars, which is reportedly close to the Iraqi insurgency, states, "The invaders, the occupiers are trying to impose their principles on Iraq. This decision is dangerous."

March 2-4. The Public Affairs Unit is continuing to prepare TV and newspaper materials on my experience in Iraq. The final video version and a newspaper publication will be coming out this upcoming Sunday. Because of this, I have been very busy. This is not only publicity about my work in Iraq and my educational and work background, but also publicity on the importance of the mission in the country. That's why many newspapers back in the States will pick up the materials, presenting them as the face of the nation's defense.

Chapter 53

New Efforts to Recruit Insurgents

March 5. Today a new online magazine created by Al-Qaida in Iraq launches an effort to recruit Muslims to rid Iraq of "infidels" and "apostates." That is what they call Americans and their Iraqi allies. This is a very well-designed and colorful magazine. It is named Zurwat As-Sanam, Arabic for "The Tip of the Camel's Hump." The name is an obvious reference among Islamic militants to the "epitome of belief and virtuous activity." The magazine gives the impression that the organization is professional, capable and really understands what they are doing. I think, along with the recruiting of new insurgents, another likely purpose of this magazine is to strengthen Al-Qaida's image as being a powerful, capable organization. The magazine consists mostly of a pledge to keep fighting and also includes a vow of fealty from Az-Zarqawi to Osama Bin Laden.

The cover of the magazine includes Al-Qaida in Iraq's logo, an AK-47 rifle standing in an open Quran, with a globe in the background and an arm and finger pointed upward. It also has pictures of President Bush, Bin Laden and Abu Anas Ash-Shami- the late spiritual leader of Al-Qaida in Iraq. Ash-Shami, a Palestinian, was a close aide to Az-Zarqawi. He was killed in a September air strike in the western suburb of Abu Ghraib in the Baghdad area. The magazine says that, "enlightening Muslims and calling upon the people to follow the faith and way of Sunnis" is its main goal. Dated February 2005, the magazine promises to continue its publications.

March 6. Today an article about my work in Iraq comes out in the military newspaper "The Anaconda Times." There is a whole page devoted to the story with my picture on it. At the same time, video newsreel about me is being played in the movie theaters of the U.S.

bases beginning today. According to the Public Affairs Unit they have also sent a copy to the major TV news stations in the U.S.

Because of the publicity, many soldiers and contractors start to recognize me wherever I go, saying that this is the "genius," which is what the newsreels and newspapers called me, referring to my work, educational background and language skills. The stories describe my work and interactions in the villages with the Civil Affairs Unit, with the Military Intelligence, and at the military convoy staging area and other activities.

March 7. We are going on a mission again. We will be visiting three villages: 14 Ramadan, Al-Betera and Al-Ouabaitar. There are projects we financially support in all three villages. All of them are almost completed. The purpose of the site visits to make sure that everything is going well and to talk to the leaders and residents of the villages. Besides, just talking to the Iraqis and listening to their needs and their problems goes a long way. I can always see in their eyes that they appreciate it, and I am sure that it will definitely pay off in the long run. This is about winning hearts and minds of the Iraqis, which is not at all less important than military and security operations in the country.

In Al-Betera village, a little boy comes up to me and asks me to give him some money. I look at him and notice that he doesn't have shoes, his feet are all in mud and dirt, and his cloth is very old and ripped. I give him money and I ask where his parents are. He says that his father died and his mother is sick. I ask him if he has brothers and sisters. He shows me a little girl standing in a distance, looking at us. He says that this is his sister and she is also hungry. I get some candies and cookies from Humvee and give them to the kids. The boy then asks me to visit his mother because she is very sick and she needs help. He shows me a quite remote house in the distance and asks me to come with him. I am about to ask my commanders for permission to go with him, but at that moment we are getting an order to leave. The mission is over. Later when I tell other people about this incident, I am told that the boy's invitation to the house might have been a trap by the insurgents. The order to leave right then may have prevented me from getting killed or taken hostage. Who knows what the reality of that situation was. I am still not sure. I frequently see those two little kids in my dreams; they look at me and beg me to come with them to their house. I go to their house and enter it. It is very dark inside. Then the boy, with the voice of an adult, tells me not to be afraid and to come. He goes inside and I follow him. At the end of the room I see a sick woman in a bed. Her eyes are closed and she is very pale. The boy tells her, "Mom, he came, open your eyes." The woman opens her big eyes and, suddenly, she asks me with coughing and scary voice, "Why are you here, why did you come to Iraq?" I look at the boy and the boy is laughing at me, but his sister is crying. Then I look at the woman. Her eyes are closed again. Usually at that moment, I wake up.

March 8. Today is International women's day, which is still widely celebrated in the former USSR, including Azerbaijan, where I am originally from.

Now I am in the internet café sending a message to my wife and daughter to congratulate them.

March 9. Very quiet day. Nothing special.

March 10. We are going out on our next mission. Heavy rains continue for several days. This is very unusual for this area. We are hardly moving in our military Humvees because we risk rolling over into canals on the sides of the muddy roads. Ahead of us Staff Sergeant G's Humvee almost slides onto the canal and the entire convoy has to stop. It is impossible to move further and we are becoming a good target for the insurgents if they decide to attack us.

Lieutenant Colonel K. makes the decision to cancel the mission and go back to the base before we are able to reach the villages.

In the evening of the same day we go with the Public Affairs representatives to the coffee shop. It is a nice place to spend some time after a difficult day.

March 11. I feel very tired today and I asked for permission to stay in the room. I write notes for this book and I do some reading. Local translator Salman asked me to correct some material in English for him. He gave me both English and Arabic materials to compare. I will probably be doing this for the rest of the day.

March 12. We go outside of the wire on a mission. It is a quick trip to Albu Fazi village; we will just pay the contractors and then come back. Albu Fazi is about a ten minute ride away from "Anaconda" air base. Lieutenant Colonel K. is negotiating with the villagers and I am translating.

On the way back to the base, we talk to our military driver. Specialist H. had been injured two times and was awarded two Purple Heart medals. Despite his injuries he volunteered to stay for a second year.

March 13. My day off. Nothing special is happening.

Chapter 54

Moving Military Convoys for Logistical Support of the Army's Operations

March 14. I am at the military convoy staging area. All military teams have been moved to a new trailer. Captain B. tells me that only we are allowed to be in that trailer, but not foreign national contractors working for the U.S. Army, because there is some classified information on the walls. I chose to be in my old place and continue to receive visitors there. It is quiet and convenient for me. I occasionally go to another office if I need something there.

Because of the rainy weather, the roads are still very muddy. Therefore, we have no plans yet to continue our outside missions for at least the entire week.

In the evening, we are planning to go to the coffee shop with Specialist T. and Specialist T. from the Public Affairs Unit. They were actively involved in preparing the video and newspaper materials about my work in Iraq. When they suggested that we have some coffee and spend time together, I gladly agreed.

Now, I am at the military convoy staging area, talking to several Arab contractors. They are sick and need medical assistance. I explain to them that we do not provide any medical services except in emergency situations. Foreign national contractors are supposed to get medical help when they return to their home countries. Unfortunately, this is an official regulation that we have to follow. Many contractors are getting upset, but there is nothing we can do about it.

While returning from work, I see that soldiers surround the area across the military store PX-BX. I come up to them and ask about the situation. They tell me that there is an unexploded rocket launched by insurgents, and the soldiers are defusing it right now.

Later, we go with Public Affairs Unit to the coffee shop, as was planned before. I am also given a DVD of the video newsreel about my work in Iraq. We talk and have a good time.

March 15. I am at the military convoy staging area. I am talking to several contractors. They are asking about the schedule of the departing military convoys. It is a very casual day. A mortar attack occurred close to a dining facility this morning. I have so much work to do that I stay in my work place after the siren sound of the alarm goes off.

March 17. I am at the military convoy staging area again. Several contractors are asking about the military convoys that are headed towards Al-Assad, though they usually go through Baghdad. We tell them that there is no information yet about the convoys in that direction. Movement in some directions is temporarily halted for security reasons.

March 18. I am at the military convoy staging area. One contractor needs help to recover his truck that was left near Tikrit, which is north of "Anaconda." We suggest that he goes to the military convoy staging area office in Tikrit, because they cover that area. We will give him a letter explaining the situation.

Later today, a local Iraqi worker on the base is caught with a map in his pocket. He was marking the distances to the public gatherings of the U.S. soldiers and contractors, particularly the dining facilities. Obviously, this map is meant to help the insurgents. Specialist K. in our Unit reminds us that the same kind of situation took place about two months ago when a local Iraqi worker blew himself up while inside of the dining facility on the U.S. base in the northern city of Mosul. There were 22 casualties, including 19 U.S. soldiers and contractors. Specialist K. and other soldiers are saying that insurgents are looking for possibilities to penetrate the bases. And it is becoming clear, after talking to the Iraqis and other contractors, that insurgents are beginning to move increasingly farther to the south. Obviously, this is happening because of the active military and security operations conducted by the U.S. and Iraqi government forces in the northern and central parts of the country.

I am getting the impression that the bridge near Talil is very dangerous. Talil is located farther to the south from the Shiite holy cities of An-Najaf and Karbala. We hear that each time the contractors pass across the bridge with the military convoys, insurgents either attack them or children throw rocks at them

March 19. While on the way to Kuwait, insurgents massively attacked our convoy with small arms fire and IEDs. One contractor-truck driver was killed and five were wounded.

Also, there is a major blockage at the North gate of the "Anaconda" air base, which frustrates the movement of the military convoys. That is one of the main reasons why the insurgents decided to attack—they probably saw a good opportunity to strike. The information that the insurgents are becoming more active in the central and southern parts of the country seems to be proving itself. We are located in the central part of Iraq, to the north of Baghdad.

Chapter 55

One Year Since I Left Home

March 20. Today marked exactly one year since I left home and headed to Fort Benning to prepare for my deployment in Iraq.

We are having a mortar attack early in the morning and a rocket attack in the evening.

March 21. Today we are going on a mission to two villages: Jamil Umran and Al-Ouabator. Water purification projects in both villages are almost completed.

However, when we arrive at Jamil Umran and talk to the representative of the village, he says that the filtration facility is not enough for the entire area; it is good enough for only one village. Although the Jamil Umran project is 80% complete and the Al-Ouabator facility is completely finished, if the villager is telling the truth, the capacity of the projects should be expanded.

Lieutenant Colonel K. tells the representative that this is what we can do at this point, but the projects might be expanded sometime in the future. On the way to Jamil Umran, we pick up Salman, our translator, at the Albu-Fazi village.

After Jamil Umran, we go to Al-Ouabator. We are having a conversation with the leader of the village. He is complaining that the project is not working, because they are having problems with the City Council. He says that when the village needs anything, the City Council is telling them to get help from the Americans because, according to the Council, Americans are sponsoring the project and they are the ones who need to provide assistance. The leader of the village says that everybody in the City Council only thinks about themselves; they don't care about the village or other people.

Lieutenant Colonel K. promises to talk to the U.S. representative at the City Council. But at the same time, he reminds them that the current policy is to encourage Iraqis to deal more with their sovereign government and less with the Americans.

While moving through the village, we see that some houses have three flags on their roofs: green, red, and black flags. Lieutenant Colonel K. is asking me about their purpose. I tell him that this is obviously a predominantly Shiite village. When he asks why I think so, I explain that all three flags have a religious meaning: green is the color of Islam, the black flag is the reflection of Shiites' mourning for their killed Imams centuries ago (as well as Hussein and others), and the red color is the symbol of revenge against those who killed their Imams. That is why I came to the conclusion that this is mainly a Shiite village. But also, I can see by the color of shumaakhs (men's national head cover), which are white and black for Shiites.

I like this village. There are always many friendly people outside, and the village is very nice, with trees, grass and home animals all around. The air is fresh and the general environment in the village is very peaceful. Both villages we are visiting today are predominantly populated by Shiites.

Now, we are returning to the base. On the way, we are stopping several times and our speed is really slow. Salman is getting upset and tells me that the frequent stops and slow speed might be very dangerous in an open area, where the insurgents are active.

Unexpectedly, Major C. stops his Humvee and approaches our Humvee, which I am riding in with Lieutenant Colonel K.

Major C. had an argument with Captain G. in the first Humvee, in which they were riding together, and he tells K. that he is not going to be with Captain G. in the same vehicle. So, we have to make some changes. I go to Captain G.'s Humvee and Major C. takes my place.

While we are approaching the base, we receive the information that a bomb was found at the South gate. Therefore, we have to change our route and enter through the North gate. Finally, we safely reach the base.

March 23. We are going on a mission again to two villages: Al-Anwar and Albu-Izba. Both are for water purification projects. The water filtration projects that we are trying to sponsor are very important in order to provide Iraqis with drinking water. Many Iraqis, especially in the villages, are still using water from canals, which can lead to different illnesses.

The Albu-Izba project is about 75% complete and the project in Al-Anwar is completely finished.

Lieutenant Colonel K. was upset that the Mayor of the Yastrib province Shovket is only taking care of his tribe and not the entire area.

The villagers are complaining that the projects don't have electricity, the switches to turn the water on are broken, and no chloride is provided to clean the water.

The mission was quick and we safely return to the base.

March 24. Today we are going to three villages: Ahmed Jazim, An-Nazaha, and 14 Ramadan. We have projects in all three villages. When we get to Ahmed Jazim, we learn that there are shootings nearby, about 300 meters from our location. But the villagers tell us that there is a funeral ceremony and traditionally Iraqis fire shots in the air during the funeral.

I help translate while Lieutenant Colonel K. discusses the projects with village representatives. Common problems usually include: not enough electricity to fuel generators, no chloride, broken pipes, etc. The main issue remains as to whether or not the City Council will maintain the projects after the Americans complete them.

Now we are moving to An-Nazaha for a site visit of the project. We encounter the same kind of problems that we had in the previous village.

We have a grand opening of the Water Filtration Facility in 14 Ramadan Village. According to the villagers, that project covers about 5,000 people in the area, including several villages.

Public Affairs Unit is participating in the mission. They are taking pictures and videotaping our activities. I am actively interpreting all interactions with Iraqis. The Public Affairs representative tells me that they might need my help from time to time during their missions. I tell them that I would be happy to help if other Units do not need me at the same time, because I work for many Units upon demand. It is very unpredictable as to which Unit is going to use me the next day or even the same day, because an emergency situation could always arise.

After the mission, Staff Sergeant G. tells me that when we learned earlier about the small arms fire, one of our officers stayed in the vehicle, and Lieutenant Colonel K. was looking for him. According to Sergeant G., the officer was obviously afraid of a possible attack.

March 25. I am going with Sergeant R. of the Civil Affairs Unit to exchange my body armor for a larger size. I am still waiting for the confirmation of the flight to Talil, which is scheduled for tomorrow.

March 26. I am at the military convoy staging area. Today I learn that the trip to Talil is cancelled because no aircrafts are available for that direction.

March 27. Today is my day off. I play soccer, clean my room, use computer, and read newspapers. Two U.S. soldiers and one marine were killed over the weekend. The soldiers were killed in the Baghdad area and the marine was killed in Anbar province during military operations.

March 28. I am at the military convoy staging area. I help translate and verify the Arabic signs that are on the back of the military vehicles. I also help translate for some of the Turkish construction workers.

March 29. I receive an email from my wife telling me that Colonel Z.—my former Civil Affairs Commander in Iraq—called and asked when I would be coming back to the U.S. I sent a message to Colonel Z. and received a reply from him. He told me that he was planning to move with his family to my area.

Chapter 56

The Political Process Moves Forward

March 30. It looks like the good spring weather has brought insurgent attacks in Iraq and Afghanistan up again.

Four Romanian journalists were abducted in Baghdad after interviewing Iraqi Interim Prime Minister Ayad Allawi. The Iraqi security forces and police are continuing to be targeted by insurgents. This past week has also seen U.S. casualties.

In the meantime, the Iraqi National Assembly has again failed to nominate a Speaker of the Assembly. The speaker is supposed to be a Sunni Arab, in an attempt to attract Sunni Arabs to the government and defuse the insurgency. The Current Interim President has reportedly refused to be a speaker of the Assembly.

March 31. We have one mortar attack today. After it is safe, I meet with my manager to discuss the possibility of staying for a second year. He tells me that they would like me to stay because of my excellent performance. I receive a certificate of achievement, an excellent evaluation of my work, and a 5% salary increase. The manager is also going to give me a separate letter of recommendation on my performance on Monday.

Also, he will give me the exact date that I am supposed to leave for good or for just a vacation, before returning for a second year.
April 1. Shiites heading to a major religious festival south of Baghdad are attacked by gunmen. They opened fire on the pilgrims, killing one and injuring two.

Thousands of Shiite Muslims across Iraq are heading to the Holy southern city of Karbala to celebrate the Al-Arbaeen religious festival. The festival marks the end of a 40-day mourning period for one of the most important saints, the grandson of Prophet Muhammed, Imam

Hussein, who was killed in a 7th-century battle for the power of Halif (former head of the Islamic state).

Also, insurgents attack the Mosul building of one of the leading Kurdish parties. An attacker was killed by return fire, but two guards were injured.

The negotiations among the Iraqi National Assembly members to nominate a prominent Sunni Arab as an Assembly speaker are still continuing.

Interim President Ghazi Al-Yawer, a Sunni Arab, will most likely be offered a post of one of two Vice Presidential positions.

April 4. Iraqi lawmakers elect industry minister Hajim Al-Hassani, a Sunni Arab, as a parliament speaker, ending days of deadlock and moving forward in forming a new government, two months after the country's historic elections.

In the meantime, a statement purportedly made by Al-Qaida in Iraq claims responsibility for the attack on the notorious Abu Ghraib jail. During the attack on the jail, which is located in the west of Baghdad, 44 U.S. service members and 12 prisoners are injured. According to the statement, about 39 Katyusha rockets were fired at U.S. forces before militants detonated several suicide car bombs at the prison's main gates. Some U.S. soldiers are evacuated with serious injuries.

April 5-6. Four U.S. soldiers were killed during the last two days. The Interim President of Iraq is elected as one of the Vice Presidents by the Iraqi National Assembly. Jalal Talabani, the Kurdish leader, is expected to become President.

April 7-8. According to the *Associated Press*, April 6 marks 1,543 U.S. military casualties.

In the meantime, the political process is moving forward. Iraq's Presidential council was sworn in on Thursday. Jalal Talabani, the former Kurdish rebel leader, has become Iraq's President. He has two deputies: one is a Shiite Arab and the second is former Interim President Ghazi Al-Yawer. The Presidential council named Shiite Arab Ibrahim

Al-Jaafari to the country's most powerful position—Interim Prime Minister—giving Iraq its first freely elected government in fifty years.

Some have expressed concern about Al-Jaafari's close ties to Iran and his work for Iraq's first Shiite Islamic political party –the Islamic Dawa Party. However, the lawmakers did not express any of those reservations on Thursday. Al-Jaafari spent more than two decades in exile, mostly in Britain and Iran, helping to lead anti-Saddam opposition forces in the Islamic Dawa party. He also has close ties to Grand Ayatollah Ali As-Sistani, Iraq's most influential Shiite cleric. Al-Jaafari's wife is a distant relative of As-Sistani. Hajim Al-Hassani, formerly one of the Interim ministers, became a Parliament speaker.

April 9. Today is a huge anti-American demonstration in Baghdad, demanding U.S. troops to withdraw from Iraq.

In the morning, we are going on our next mission to two villages: Ahmed Jasim and An-Nazaha. We have water purification projects in both villages.

In Ahmed Jasim, Iraqi contractors tell us that they have not been paid yet by the U.S. Army for their work with the projects. But Major C. says that in accordance with the official invoice from the Army's command, the contractors have already been paid $80,000. Major C. promises to research the issue again and give the contractors more precise information.

In An-Nazaha, we talk to village children and representatives about their needs. Children ask us to bring a soccer ball when we come next time.

The main problem facing the projects in both villages is the shortage of power for the facilities' generators.

April 10. Today is my day off. Our soccer team is growing and more and more soldiers and contractors are joining it. There were just a few players when I first started it. The Public Affairs Unit representatives also play with us and prepare material about our team for publication in the military newspapers.

Chapter 57

Dangerous Mission

April 11. Today I am asked to go with Lieutenant Colonel D. and Major B. from the engineering Unit to the volatile Diyala province. The Diyala, Anbar, and Babil provinces are considered to be some of the most dangerous places in Iraq. A local interpreter named Eva, who is a Christian Arab, was supposed to go with the Unit for this mission. However, because she is from the Diyala province and the people there know her, it would be too dangerous. I am also warned that the mission is not ordinary and quite risky. I agree to go, anyway. Eva has already been shot and wounded before. She and her family are going through a difficult period because of their work for the coalition forces.

During the mission, our security is provided by the special attachment of contractors from the South African Republic, Britain, and the U.S. We are driving in three SUVs. I am riding in the middle SUV with Lieutenant Colonel D. and Major B. In our vehicle, the security is provided by Pier and Justin. Both of them are from the South African Republic, athletically built and very professional security agents. B. tells me that the security agents are primarily former special police forces in their respective countries.

First we go to the Al-Qaim elementary primary school, which is located in a remote area of the Diyala province. We have to drive to another side of the Tigris River for the first time. It is quite a long ride. We meet with teachers and children and give them some school supplies. There are complaints about a lack of functional classrooms and overcrowding in the classrooms. The representatives of the school ask us to help with repairing the school and adding new classrooms. They say that U.S. Army personnel and representatives from the Iraqi

Ministry of Education have come in the past, but have done little to help the school. Lieutenant Colonel D. promises to talk to the U.S. representatives about the issue.

Now we are heading towards the second school, Muhammed Abdo. We get lost on the way. This is a huge desert area and we are a perfect target for the insurgents. We see a group of Iraqis working in the field next to the road. We decide to approach them and ask for directions. I go up to them and first ask about their families and children. In other words, I am trying to initiate contact by first considering their cultural peculiarities. Then, I explain that we are lost and need help with directions. They show us the way to the main road leading to the school. The Iraqis also tell us to be careful in the area because there was an explosion at the voting station in the Al-Qaim school three days before the elections.

We finally arrive at Muhammed Abdo and meet with the school's guards and representatives from the village. They complain that an assigned contractor comes occasionally, takes money, but does little or no work. They also complain about the power shortage, which is only giving off seven kilowatts of electricity for forty houses.

The school is in such terrible shape that the villagers tell us that the classes are being held outside in the yard.

Now we are leaving the village and going back towards the base. Although the security guys use a computer device to direct our way, we are lost again. While trying to find our way out, we see very interesting natural caves in the middle of the desert. Finally, we manage to get to the main road. Major B. shows me the camp, which is called Al-Ashraf. It is located closer to the Iranian border. During the Saddam Hussein era, the so-called Iranian "Mujaheddin Al-Khalq group" was given refuge in Iraq because the group strongly opposes the Iranian government and is actively trying to change it. I also heard from Iraqis that the organization fought on the Iraqi side during the Iraq-Iran war. I am pleased to have passed this area, which is full of history and politics.

We safely return to the base. I am asked to join them for the next mission to Kirkush on Saturday, but it still has to be confirmed, depending on the security situation.

April 12. Today I am at the military convoy staging area. One contractor asks us to help recover his truck that had broken down on a Baghdad road on the way to Zakhu. Zakhu is located in the northern Kurdish areas. Turkey was supposed to be his final destination.

April 13. Today is our next mission with my Civil Affairs Unit. We are going to the Albu Hassan village for our water purification project.

First, we stop at the village's elementary school and talk to its director, teachers, and students. The school is in very good shape, but the school's officials wish that three to four additional class rooms could be added to the main facility.

After some negotiations with the representatives of the village, Sheikh Waadi, who is responsible for the area, invites us to his quest house, which is located next to the water purification facility. There, we meet Sheikh's daughter, and she warmly greets us. She is just back from school. I am told that it will soon be time for her to put her headscarf on; the pre-marriage age is nearing. Lieutenant Colonel K., Major C., our local translator Salman Saffe, and I are invited into a big room, which obviously serves as a leaving room. It is decorated with many religious writings, including the names of all twelve Shiite Imams, starting with Imam Ali and ending with Imam Mehdi. This is obviously a Shiite family; Sheikh Waadi put his shumaakh (national headscarf) on while talking to us. We have a long conversation with the Sheikh on different issues related to the village and the project.

After a bit, Sheikh Waadi invites us to the next room to have lunch with him and his people. The Iraqi food is delicious and was brought from downtown Balad especially for this occasion. We particularly like Iraqi "kama," which naturally grows on the ground after the rain. It looks like a meat but is probably a vegetable. Then we have salads, chicken, BBQ of beef and lamb, and in the end—as usual—we are served tea mixed with sugar in small glasses.

During the entire mission, the security was provided by our own Unit and soldiers from other Units as well.

While we are in the house, Staff Sergeant G. comes in several times, reminding us that it is time to leave because it is dangerous to stay in one place for a lengthy time. The soldiers who are guarding the outside are also were very hot inside of the Humvees.

We successfully complete our mission and safely return to the base.

Chapter 58

Violence Escalates and the First Elected Government is Formed

April 16-17. Violence escalated over the weekend. Two U.S. marines were killed on Saturday. Eleven inmates escaped from U.S. camp "Bucca", but ten of them were later captured.

In the south of Baghdad, about 100 insurgents take approximately 80 residents hostage in Madain, a city of mixed Shiite and Sunni population. The insurgents threaten to kill hostages if the Shiites don't leave the city.

In the meantime, the formation of the Interim government is still underway. Interim President Jalal Talabani suggests that Iraqi insurgents might be amnestied, but not foreign fighters. Also, violence occurs in different parts of Iraq over the week.

April 18-20. Violence in Baghdad against Iraqi police and security forces is still continuing. A U.S. based human rights organization representative is among the dead. There is no new information available about the American hostage Ake.

In the meantime, the last Iraqi inmate among those who escaped from the U.S. detention camp was captured.

April 21-22. A Russian-made helicopter was shot down by insurgents. As a result, six U.S. Blackwater security company employees, three Bulgarians, and two Fijians were killed. Al-Jazeera aired footage of the burned helicopter and showed how the only survivor was repeatedly shot by insurgents. He was lying on the ground when the voice of a cameraman commanded him to get up. The man said in heavily-accented English that his leg was broken and stretched out his hand, asking for help. Then he was helped to stand up and was commanded to go. He tried to walk and then turned towards his captors, apparently trying to say "no" to whatever his captors were doing. The insurgents then shot him repeatedly, even when he had already collapsed, shouting "Allahu Akbar" (God is Great) in Arabic as he went down. The footage claimed that it was revenge for the killed Muslims in Fallujah mosques, apparently referring to last November's U.S. assault on the city of Fallujah, and particularly to the incident when a wounded Iraqi man was killed by a U.S. marine.

Nine people are killed inside a Shiite mosque and approximately 50 bodies are fished out from the Tigris River; they are apparently the bodies of hostages taken by Sunni insurgents in Madain.

On April 22, I am stopped by a U.S. military police soldier without any reason, while walking from the dining facility with Salman. The policeman tells me that my badge should be visible all the time. He sees my look of surprise and repeatedly asks me, "Your badge was not on your neck, you put it later, am I right? Am I right?" Having realized that the situation is not in my favor and I will not be able to prove anything to that angry armed soldier, I reply, "Yes sir, you are right." But in fact, the badge was always on my neck and I never touched it. Salman is very surprised and says to me, "He called with his finger when he stopped his car and I thought that he was going to say that he had seen you on the movie," referring to the newsreel about me that the Army started to air since recently. Salman jokingly says, "If you had blue eyes, he never would have done it. You need to wear blue contact lenses." Salman sadly tells me that after I leave, it will be very difficult for him, in terms of morale, and he will probably quit.

Later in the evening, Staff Sergeant G., Salman and I are having a conversation. G. says that the U.S. came to Iraq and invaded it, but didn't find any weapons of mass destruction. He thinks that a real reason for the invasion was Iraqi oil. He suggests that the U.S. wouldn't like it if some Muslim country invaded it. And equally, our invasion of a Muslim country is not right. He says that there is a lack of understanding of Muslim culture and religion. As an example, he recalled his conversation with Lieutenant Colonel K., when G. told K. that he was a Muslim. In reply, K. asked G. if he had a card or some kind of paper proving that G. was a Muslim; that question deeply offended G. He says that K. is a Christian—does that mean that he is supposed to have some kind of card proving it? G. decided not to talk about that topic with K. anymore. Later, Sergeant G. asked me to mention this incident in my future book.

April 23. I meet a soldier in the bathroom area. He asks me where I am originally from. He keeps asking me, "Are you from India?" I reply, "No." "Are you from Pakistan?" I reply, "No." Finally, he remembers that we have met before and that I am from the U.S. After that, his attitude drastically changes and he starts talking to me like I am an equal. He asks me with a confident voice if I understand what is going on in Iraq. Then he answers his own question by saying that the Satan is making Iraqi people to fight each other, and until the Jesus Christ gets into the souls of Muslims, the violence will not stop. He also says that God is with Israel and the Jews and that is why Arabs and Palestinians cannot do anything against them. According to that soldier, everybody hates Americans—Indians, Pakistanis, Arabs—and the main reason for their hatred is that Satan has settled in their souls. The soldier continues, saying that the Jews and Americans can fight Satan. In the end, he says that is why he is in Iraq. But it is not clear to me exactly what he means by that. Does he mean that he is in Iraq to help to fight Satan and make sure that Jesus gets into the souls of those Muslim people? I am still not sure.

The soldiers in my Unit tell me that they will miss me when I leave. I tell them that I am going to miss them as well. They have really become like a family for me.

April 24. Today is my day off. Eight days are left before I leave home after being in Iraq for one year.

April 25-30. Prime Minister Ibrahim Al-Jaafari finally submits his partial list of cabinet members to President Jalal Talabani for approval. After the President's endorsement, Iraq's Interim National Assembly approves the partial list of ministers on Thursday. This finally takes place after almost three months of political debates. However, two key positions in the 37-member government—defense and oil—remain disputed, mainly because of an attempt to incorporate the Sunni Arab minority and doubts about the membership of many of them in Saddam Hussein's former Baath party.

The main government positions are given to the following politicians:

Ibrahim Al-Jaafari is a Prime Minister and acting Defense Minister. Al-Jaafari, 57, whose real name is Ibrahim Al-Shukair, is a senior member in the Shiite Dawa party, which ran one of the main Iraqi armed groups that tried to topple Saddam Hussein's Baath regime. He fled Iraq in 1980 after a crackdown on the party. In Iran, he was engaged in political activities in the ranks of the Dawa party. The group's militia carried out attacks on Iraq during the 1980-1988 Iraq-Iran war. He later left for Syria, then to the United Kingdom. He returned to Iraq after Saddam's fall in 2003 and was a member of the Governing Council.

Ahmad Chalabi is a Deputy Prime Minister and acting Oil Minister. In 1958, Chalabi, 58 left Iraq and became one of the most prominent figures of the Iraqi opposition in exile, forming close ties with the Pentagon and actively lobbying to remove Saddam Hussein from power. After the former regime's fall, he became a member of the Governing Council and was thought by some politicians in Washington as the potential future leader of Iraq.

Hoshyar Zebari is a Foreign Minister. Zebari, 55, belongs to a powerful Kurdish tribe in northwest Iraq. He is an uncle of Massoud Barzani, one of the two leaders who control the Kurdish areas. He was a spokesman for Barzani's Kurdish Democratic Party, where he was active in opposition contacts with the United States before the war. He has held the Foreign Minister's post since the first interim government was formed in June 2004.

Bayan Jabr, 55, is an Interior Minister. He was a Shiite activist while studying engineering at Baghdad University in the 1970s. He fled to Iran amid a Saddam crackdown on Shiite political groups and joined the Supreme Council of the Islamic Revolution in Iraq. After the former regime's fall, he became the Minister of Housing and Reconstruction in the first provisional government.

Ali Abdel-Amir Allawi is a Finance Minister. Allawi, a wealthy businessman, was previously a consultant to the World Bank, and he heads a London based investment company called Pan Arab. He was elected to the Iraqi National Assembly on the United Iraqi Alliance ticket. Ali Allawi left Iraq in 1956 for Britain, which is where he went to high school.

Former Interim Prime Minister Ayad Allawi's Iraqi List Party is not included in the new Cabinet.

The approved ministers include 15 Shiite Arabs, seven Kurds, four Sunnis, and one Christian. Lawmakers intend to give two more ministries for Shiites, one for Kurds, and two for Sunnis. The government includes six women, responsible for seven portfolios.

President Jalal Talabani and his two Vice Presidents signed off on the list before Thursday's historic vote.

Of the 26 million Iraqi citizens, 60% are Shiites, 20% are Kurds, and about 15-20% are Sunni Arabs.

An official handover between outgoing Prime Minister Ayad Allawi and incoming Ibrahim Al-Jaafari is expected within the next days. The decision about the two vacant Prime Minister slots and five acting Ministerial positions will be made in three to four days.

In the meantime, a wave of insurgent attacks has escalated in recent days. A new videotape by Al-Qaida leader Abu-Musaib Az-Zarqawi calls for more attacks against the U.S. and coalition forces. Obviously, the insurgency in Iraq is targeting the new government, hoping to return the lost power and privileges.

But, it looks like that there is no unified nationalistic element directed against the U.S. and the coalition forces, which was the case in Algeria in the 1950s against the French. That scenario would have been much more complicated for Washington.

Those international fighters who are ideologically motivated and more sophisticated present the most challenge and danger for the new Iraqi government and coalition forces. But if the tactics of the insurgents continue to be as they have been so far, the increasingly stronger Iraqi security forces, combined with the frustration of the ordinary Iraqis who are paying the price for the attacks from another side, will eventually create very unfavorable ground for the insurgency in the country. In this case, the insurgency in Iraq might be gradually diminishing and can ultimately be defeated.

April 30. I am talking to Specialist G., who is a nice young person. Before coming to Iraq and working with Civil Affairs Unit, he used to serve in the Military Intelligence Unit.

He says that the U.S. administration is also planning to invade Iran. And if it happens, the U.S. will eventually win, but it would be much more difficult than in the case of Iraq. In that scenario, Iran is likely to use chemical weapons against the U.S. troops, leading to a very high number of casualties. G. also thinks that Iran would try to send troops inside of Iraq.

I am listening to G., and in my mind I agree with him. I think that the invasion of Iran would be much more difficult than Iraq for several reasons. First, Iran is a more unified country with very strong anti-American sentiments. The Iranians still remember the U.S.'s involvement in the 1953 coup and other situations in the past. Secondly, Iran has developed a strong army that is equipped with advanced technology, chemical, and biological weapons; it can also acquire nuclear capabilities in the future, as well. In fact, it is believed that the country is actively pursuing these plans.

Chapter 59

Preparing To Go Home

May 1-3. I am in Baghdad for processing in connection with my resignation and expected departure back to the U.S. Before I left, I met Majid at the airfield in Balad. We were together at the Conus Replacement Center at Fort Benning one year ago. At that time, he decided to postpone his work with the U.S. Army, out of fear for the safety of his family, who still lived in Iraq's second largest city of Basra. Majid was particularly fearful because of the Shiite uprising led by Muqtada As-Sadr and the possibility that Majid's family could be targeted. Now, one year later, I am going home after completing my mission in Iraq, but Majid is only beginning his assignment. He tells me that he has come to Iraq for the first time in fifteen years since he fled the country.

We board the military helicopter together and head towards Baghdad. While flying, Majid is looking down and I can see that his eyes are full of tears.

It is a beautiful view of Baghdad from the helicopter. It takes us about forty minutes until we finally land at the "Griffin" military airfield.

Today is the second day I am in Baghdad, staying at Saddam's former Zoo in one of his former palaces. Other military contractors are also staying there. My military ID card has expired, and I am waiting to get a new one to be able to travel. From Baghdad, I am supposed to go back to Balad, which is located to the north. From Balad, I will fly to Germany and from Germany to Fort Benning, in order to turn in my military equipment. Fort Benning will be my final destination before I leave for home. Then, I will board the civilian plane going to Washington DC. I expect to be home by the end of this week.

May 4. I am waiting for the military helicopter flight back to Balad. I spent all of yesterday working on getting a new military ID.

About 30 new Army linguists have arrived. Some of them are talking about the possibility that a contract for the Army linguists might not be renewed anytime soon, because U.S. troops and coalition forces might start withdrawing from Iraq. Personally, I don't believe that our troops are going to leave the country any time soon.

I decided to walk to my place after finally getting my new ID. But, I get lost on the way and have no idea how to get to my area. Luckily, I see one of the defense contractors who is also driving towards the same place. She gives me a ride and I realize that the distance between my location and the area I am staying in is much greater than I thought; I would not have been able to make it by walking.

Most of the linguists are going to Fallujah and Ramadi, which are located in the volatile Anbar province. At least one linguist is heading towards the southern city of Najaf.

On the same day, I finally come back to the "Anaconda" base in Balad and go to my manager's office for the final preparations. T. tells me to be ready for the 2:45 pm flight to Germany.

Everybody at the Civil Affairs Unit thought that I had already left. Sergeant R. is very happy to see me. He tells me that Salman also thought that I had left and was very upset.

Sergeant R. takes us to CIF (military warehouse) to return my armor vest. After that, we decide to go to the dining facility to have a lunch. There, we meet the soldiers from another Civil Affairs Unit. They already know that I am leaving soon and they tell me that they are going to miss me. Specialist S., their Iraqi translator Eva, and others wish me good luck, and we agree to keep in touch. Eva says that she regrets that she will probably never see me again. She is really nice, and I sincerely hope that her and her family will stay safe.

I start packing as soon as I arrive at my place.

Troy comes to pick me up. I say goodbye to my Unit. Commander

Lieutenant Colonel K. warmly sees me off and tells me that he might be coming to my area in the U.S. and would like to meet with me. I reply that it would be great and give him my address and phone number. It was an emotional farewell, because the danger of war has made us like a family. I see such sadness and tears in the eyes of my fellow soldiers. And I feel the same way. R. is the last soldier to see me off. Before I get in the car, we hug each other and promise to keep in touch and meet in the U.S. And eventually, after he completes his mission in Iraq, we will meet. R's eyes are clearly wet; I turn my head away because I am also becoming emotional at this moment.

I am leaving for Germany at about 5:00 pm on May 4, 2005 in the military plane heading to "Main Rain" U.S. air base in Frankfurt. I am writing these notes while on the plane. My year-long deployment in Iraq has come to an end today, May 4, 2005. I have been in the country for exactly one year and four days.

I stay in Frankfurt, Germany for two days in a hotel that is close to the "Main Rain" air base.

G., from my employer company, says that I made the right decision in coming back to my family after one year of service in Iraq. He also mentions that they put a recommendation to rehire me in my internal file, if I ever want to come back to Iraq or any other place as their employee. He tells me that the recommendation is based on my excellent performance, and the rehiring process would be very simplified and quick.

May 7. Today I arrive at Fort Benning for further processing and the final return of my military equipment.

May 8. I am staying in the Army barracks at Fort Benning while I complete my final processing before flying home. I meet another linguist who is coming back to Iraq from his vacation. R. works with Navy Seals in Iraq for special operations. He is a U.S. citizen of Lebanese origin. R. tells me that he was recently divorced, has four children, and owes $ 90,000.

Because of all these personal problems, he has to go back to Iraq to earn money to be able to support his children and pay his debts. Now, he is hesitating about whether to go back home to his children or to return to Iraq. According to R., the situation in Iraq is not improving and the insurgency is getting more active and sophisticated. He also thinks that the way the situation is being handled in Iraq is not right and it is not leading to positive results. As an example, he says that nobody can control the main road leading to the Baghdad International Airport and violence occurs there on a daily basis. According to him, the authorities are not being objective about the situation, especially when briefing the public. However, he thinks that as time passes and more and more wounded soldiers return to the States, more information will surface and be made available for the American public. When that happens, Americans will become increasingly frustrated by how mishandled the war has been from the very beginning.

May 9. At 5:45 am I am ready to turn in my military duffle bags. By noon, I complete all the procedures and get a receipt with a red stamp on it to show that I have returned all my military equipment to the Army.

My employer representative is ready to take me to the airport, but I ask to stay for a while to complete my medical check-up before I finally leave.

May 10. I have a 7 am appointment to go for a medical check-up. It is advisable to do this to make sure that everything is OK with my health before I get home.

Later, we are finally at our employer's office in Columbus to complete the final paperwork and get a travel itinerary. I have some free time and call my wife. She says that both her and our daughter will meet me at Dallas International Airport. I am writing these notes as I wait for my flight to arrive at 8:05 pm in Washington DC. The flight was quite smooth. I arrive at the destination as scheduled. My wife and daughter rush to me as soon as I come out of the passengers' waiting are. It is a happy and emotional meeting. The one year, four days and two hours of danger and excitement that I spent on tour in Iraq is over. It was a really unique life experience to add to my background. Finally, I am home with my family. It is good to be home.